Contents

Introduction   5

On land   6

The legend of *Bluebird*   7

Thrusting through the sound barrier   10

Wacky racers   14

Land Speed Records   15

On two wheels   18

Dragster racing   22

On the ice   25

On the water   26

In the air   29

SPEED

Simon Page and Mark Warner

Series Editors: Steve Barlow and Steve Skidmore

Published by Heinemann Educational Publishers
Halley Court, Jordan Hill, Oxford OX2 8EJ
A division of Reed Educational and Professional Publishing Ltd

OXFORD   MELBOURNE   AUCKLAND
JOHANNESBURG   BLANTYRE   GABORONE
IBADAN   PORTSMOUTH NH (USA)   CHICAGO

© Simon Page and Mark Warner, 2001
Original illustrations © Heinemann Educational Publishers, 2001

05 04 03 02 01
10 9 8 7 6 5 4 3 2 1
ISBN 0 435 21493 4

Photos: pages 8–9 – Hulton Getty; pages 10–11 – Popperfoto; pages 18–19 – Popperfoto;
pages 22–23 – Stone; pages 26–27 – Popperfoto; page 30 – TRH Pictures.
Cover design by Shireen Nathoo Design
Cover photos by: J. Davey
Designed by Artistix, Thame, Oxon
Printed and bound in Great Britain by Biddles Ltd

Tel: 01865 888058 www.heinemann.co.uk

Fast is fun

Most people enjoy the thrill of speed. From going downhill on your bike to riding the roller-coaster, speed can be exciting.

Drag car racer

> Pushing a rocket car to its limits … is a real good kick. It kinda keeps me going, you know?

But speed can kill

But speed is more than fun for some people. They spend most of their time and money trying to go fast. They can even end up dead.

First man to fly through the sound barrier

> There are at least a dozen ways that the X1 plane can kill you, so your concentration is total.

The need for speed

Read about the people who have to be the fastest, whatever the cost.

Ayrton Senna, Grand Prix World Champion 1988, 1990 and 1991

> I am not designed to come second or third. I am designed to win.

Senna died in a crash at Imola, Italy, in 1994.

On land

It takes guts to drive a car faster than anyone else. The fastest drivers become heroes. The greatest prize for them is the Land Speed Record.

The Land Speed Record

The first Land Speed Record was set in 1898. The car was electric and reached a speed of 39mph (63.15km/h). Since then the record has been broken over 60 times. It now stands at an amazing 763mph (1227.952km/h).

The rules

The driver must drive over the course twice, in opposite directions. This is in case wind-speed helps the speed of the car. The driver has one hour to do the two runs. The average speed from both runs is taken.

Wacky World Records

Norman Breedlove, USA

His jet-powered car *Spirit of America* spun out of control. He missed the Land Speed Record but set a new one – for the longest ever skid marks! They were nearly six miles (9.5km) long.

The legend of Bluebird

Sir Malcolm Campbell broke the Land Speed Record nine times. The cars he drove were all called *Bluebird*.

Bluebird Factfile

The driver

Name:	Sir Malcolm Campbell
Born:	1885 in Kent, England
Records:	Nine World Land Speed Records
	Three World Water Speed Records

The greatest moment

The 1930s were an exciting time for speed freaks. Drivers from Britain and America risked their lives trying to break the 300mph barrier.

Campbell took *Bluebird* to America in 1935. He powered *Bluebird* to a speed of 301mph (484km/h).

This was the fifth time Campbell had broken the record. He gave up Land Speed racing but went on to break the Water Speed Record three times.

Sir Malcolm Campbell died in 1948. His son Donald took up the challenge. His life was full of breaking records on land and water. It was also a story of crashes and broken bones.

Crash landing

On 16th September 1960, Donald tried to break the 400mph barrier. The record had stood at 394mph since 1947.

On the first run he reached a speed of well over 300mph. He tried to go faster on the second run. There was a terrible crash. At 365mph the car skidded and went into a spin. It flipped over four times before stopping. Campbell had a cracked skull. He was lucky to be alive.

Breaking the record

Donald Campbell would not give up. He rebuilt the car to make it stay steady at high speed. He took it to Australia. On 17th July 1964 he drove *Bluebird* to a new World Land Speed Record of 403mph (648km/h).

He had followed his father into the history books. But that is not the end of his story. Find out what happened to him in the chapter 'On the water'.

Did you know?

At full speed, *Bluebird's* engine would start to fall apart after just three minutes!

Donald Campbell in Bluebird

Thrusting through the sound barrier

- The most amazing car ever built is *Thrust SSC*.

- SSC is short for Supersonic Car.

- In October 1997 the car was driven by Andy Green. He set a new Land Speed Record of 763mph (1227km/h).

- Green also became the only man ever to break the sound barrier in a car. This was something many people thought could never be done.

The sound barrier is the speed at which sound travels. To break the sound barrier, a car must travel faster than the speed of sound.

At sea level, sound travels at a speed of between 750mph (1206.7 km/h) and 765mph (1231km/h). As the speed of sound is reached, there is a very loud bang. This is called a sonic boom.

Thrust SSC

The owner

Thrust SSC is owned by Richard Noble. It took him years of hard work to build a car that could go through the sound barrier.

The driver

Andy Green used to fly jet planes in the Royal Air Force. He was chosen because he was used to travelling at supersonic speeds.

The car

Thrust SSC was designed by a guided missile expert. It had parachutes to slow it down at the end of the run.

The place

The record was set in the Black Rock Desert in Nevada, USA. The course was on a dried-out lake bed. It was about 19 miles long.

Did you know?

There are very few places left in the world for Land Speed Record runs. The cars simply go too fast! Britain has nowhere flat and long enough for these cars to run.

Through the sound barrier

Andy Green set off on the first run. The car skimmed across the ground with a huge tail of dust behind it. A few seconds later there was a loud cracking noise. It was a sonic boom. *Thrust* had broken the sound barrier! History had been made. Now the car had to make a second run.

Drama

During the first run the car overshot the course by a mile and a half. The team only had an hour to turn it round for the second run. It took them 61 minutes. Green broke the sound barrier again but the record could not stand. He had to make a third run.

Third time lucky

Thrust set off again. This time there was no mistake. Green went through sound barrier again and smashed the Land Speed Record.

Wacky World Records

Goran Eliason, Sweden

Became a record breaker when he drove a Volvo car at a speed of 112mph (181km/h) – on two wheels!

Wacky racers

Some people just can't do things the easy way. Here is a Top Ten of the wackiest racers in the world … and all of them are World Record holders.

Jay Edington, from America, raced to a speed of 75.14km/h (46.69mph) on roller-skates … going backwards!

Rock Griffiths, from America, drove 402 metres in 16.058 seconds, reaching a record speed of 141km/h (85.47mph) … in a hearse.

Pierre Tardival, from France, became a record-breaker when he skied 3,200 metres down Mount Everest. It took him three hours.

Jack Smith, from America, took 26 days to travel across America. It doesn't sound very fast but it is a World Record … for going across the USA on a skateboard!

Mark Kenny, from America, ran 50 metres in 16.93 seconds. A World Record? Yes, it is – for running on your hands!

Land Speed Records

The Land Speed Record is under attack from at least four teams at the moment. If you'd like to learn more, type **land speed records** into Yahoo or another search engine and surf the net!

Car   *Spirit of America*

Driver Craig Breedlove

Breedlove last held the record in 1965 and wants it back for America. Find out more on **www.spiritofamerica.com**

Car   *Aussie Invader*

Driver Rosco McGlashen

Find out more on **http://invader.iinet.net.au/**

Car   *Sonic Wind*

Driver Waldo Stakes

Another American, in a rocket on skates! More on **www.geocities.com/MotorCity/Downs/3779**

Car   *North American Eagle*

Details Has a new look – like a jet fighter with the wings taken off. More on **www.landspeed.com**

Land Speed Record holders

Date	Driver	Country
18 December 1898	Gaston Chasseloup-Laubat	France
5 August 1902	William K Vanderbilt	USA
4 June 1914	LG Hornsted	UK
29 March 1927	Henry Segrave	UK
3 September 1935	Sir Malcolm Campbell	UK
17 July 1964	Donald Campbell	UK
15 November 1965	Craig Breedlove	USA
4 October 1983	Richard Noble	UK
15 October 1997	Andy Green	UK

Car	Location	Speed
Jeantaud	Achères, France	39mph (63km/h)
Mors	Ablis, France	76mph (123km/h)
Benz	Brooklands, UK	124mph (199km/h)
Sunbeam	Daytona Beach, USA	203mph (327km/h)
Bluebird	Bonneville Salt Flats, USA	301mph (484km/h)
Bluebird	Lake Eyre, Australia	403mph (648km/h)
Spirit of America Sonic 1	Bonneville Salt Flats, USA	600mph (966km/h)
Thrust 2	Black Rock Desert, USA	633mph (1019km/h)
Thrust SSC	Black Rock Desert, USA	763mph (1227km/h)

Who is the fastest man on two wheels?

An Englishman called Richard Brown.

So he holds the world record then?

No.

Why not?

Sometimes the record books do not tell the whole story...

The Mach Three Challenger. Nothing has ever gone faster on two wheels.

The story of the Rocketman

In 1999 Richard Brown went to America. He wanted to become the fastest man on two wheels. His crew was made up of part-time helpers. They had taken time off from work to help him. They were fans who had paid for their own travel. The team only had two weeks to break the record.

The bike

Brown's bike was called the *Mach Three Challenger*. He had built it himself. It was very different from other bikes. It was powered by rockets and was over eight metres long!

Getting ready

It took days to get the bike ready for the first run. The rockets worked perfectly. The problem was which tyres to use. Metal tyres were fast but caused the bike to skid. Rubber tyres were safer but slower. Finally the team chose the rubber tyres.

Running out of time!

With only a few days left, strong winds and rain held things up. The team did not want to go home without having a go at the record.

The record attempt

Luckily the weather got better. The team got the bike ready. Everything went well on the first run. Brown raced the bike at a speed of over 340mph (544km/h). If he could do this again, he would break the record. Then disaster struck. One of the tyres burst and there was not enough time to change it. The record attempt was over.

The fastest ever

His name is not in the record books – yet! But Richard 'Rocketman' Brown has driven faster on two wheels than anyone else in history.

So who does hold the record?

The World Two-Wheel Speed Record

Record holder:	Dave Campos, USA
Year:	1990
Speed:	322mph (518km/h)
Bike:	Harley Davidson called *Easyriders*. It was 23 feet (7.01 metres) long.

Wacky World Records

Patrick Furstenhoff, Sweden

Drove his motor-bike at a speed of 191mph (307km/h) – on one wheel!

Dragster racing

What is Dragster racing?

The idea is to go as fast as possible in the shortest possible time. There are no rules. It is just a matter of GO!

Two cars race each other from a standing start down a 400-metre track. They can go from 0 to 150mph (240km/h) in seconds.

Did you know?

The fastest Dragster driver of all time is Sammy Miller. His Mustang RFC car had skis instead of front wheels. It was also powered by rockets.

Acceleration

Acceleration is how quickly a car increases speed. It is what drag racing is all about. The Mustang RFC accelerated at an amazing rate.

> 0–60mph (96km/h) in 0.2sec
> 0–100mph (160km/h) in 0.3sec
> 0–288mph (464km/h) in 1sec

Miller reached a top speed of 386mph (617km/h). He had to wear a pressure suit, just like a jet-plane pilot!

Joe Gouger – born to race

Who is Joe Gouger?

Joe Gouger (*Gow-jer*) comes from a racing family. His father was a World Champion stock-car racer. As a little boy, Joe would watch all his father's races. He dreamed of racing like his Dad.

What happened to him?

Joe took up Dragster racing. He now races against all the top Dragster racers in America. Joe's best time is 145mph (232km/h) in 9.3 seconds. He is very fast.

What is special about Joe?

When Joe was 17, he broke his neck in a motor-bike crash. He cannot use his legs or his fingers. He uses a wheelchair. But Joe carries on racing. His friend, Andy Smith, lifts Joe into his car.

'He's my arms and legs,' says Joe.

How good is Joe?

Very good. Joe has raced in the National Championships. He is the first person in a wheelchair to become a top Dragster Racer. Joe shows what you can do if you put your mind to it. A friend says:

'I think he's got more heart than ten racers put together.'

On the ice

Ice can be very fast, but it is also dangerous. It is very easy to spin out of control and crash.

It is possible that the next Land Speed Record will be set on ice. Waldo Stakes of America is testing a car called *Sonic Wind* that runs on ice skates. He thinks it can power to 900mph (1440km/h) and smash the record.

Super sledge

Sammy Miller is not only a champion Dragster racer. He also holds the world record for speeding across ice on a sledge! He reached a speed of 247mph (397km/h) on frozen Lake George in the USA in 1981. The sledge was called *Oxygen* and was powered by two large rockets. Miller's skill kept the sledge in a straight line. One false move would have caused a terrible crash. On a bigger lake he would have gone even faster!

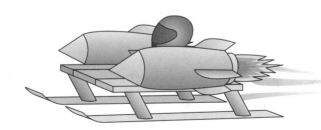

On the water

Breaking the Land Speed Record is hard. Breaking the Water Speed Record is even harder. The speeds are slower but water can be more dangerous to race on.

What happened to him?

On the first run Campbell drove *Bluebird* at over 300mph (480km/h). But he turned the boat around for the second run too quickly. He did not wait for the waves on the water to settle down. On the second run the boat lifted out of the water. It spun over in the air and crashed. His body was never found.

Was he doomed?

The night before, Campbell had told his friends that he would crash. Maybe this was why he turned the boat around so quickly. He knew that he was doomed to die.

Donald Campbell's fatal crash in 1967.

Who is the fastest man on water?

Ken Warby. He broke Donald Campbell's record in his boat, *Spirit of Australia*.

What speed did he reach?

317mph (507km/h).

How did he do it?

He did it in a home-made boat made of wood! The jet engine was second-hand. He bought it from the air-force for just $65.

Wacky World Record

Greg Mutton, Australia

Set a world record in New South Wales, Australia in 1987.
He raced across a 36-mile stretch of water in 1 hour 22 minutes
– in a motor-powered **bath tub**!

In the air

The rocket men were the people who flew planes powered by rockets instead of jet engines.

Do rocket planes go faster than jet planes?

Yes. The fastest ever rocket plane flew at a speed of 4546mph (7272km/h) in 1967. It was flown by US pilot William Knight. No one has ever flown faster than him.

Why isn't this the Air Speed Record then?

Because rocket planes cannot take off and land on their own. They have to be dropped from the air by a huge bomber.

The crew of the American jet plane *Blackbird* hold the record. It reached a speed of 2193mph (3508km/h) in 1976.

Did you know?

The first Air Speed Record was set in November 1906 in France. The plane flew at 25mph (40km/h). It was another 15 years before aircraft could go as fast as trains!

Chuck Yeager - the danger man

Who is he?

Chuck Yeager *(Yay-ger)* is the most famous of all the rocket plane pilots. In 1947 he became the first man to break the sound barrier.

Was it dangerous?

Yes, very. Many test pilots were killed when they tried to fly at high speed. In 1952, 62 American pilots were killed in just 36 weeks.

The Bell X1 *flown by Captain 'Chuck' Yeager.*

Where was it done?

At the Edwards air base, which was named after a dead test pilot. All the roads around the base were named after dead pilots, too!

Why was Chuck Yeager chosen?

He was a fighter pilot in the war. Although he suffered from air sickness, he shot down 13 German planes!

How did he break the sound barrier?

Chuck flew a small plane called the *Bell X1*. It was shaped like a machine-gun bullet. It was carried into the sky by a B-29 bomber and then dropped. The plane's rockets were fired and it zoomed upwards. Chuck kept going until he heard a loud noise. It was a sonic boom. He had gone through the sound barrier.

How brave was he?

Very brave. He broke two ribs in a fall the day before the flight. The doctor told him not to fly for two months! Chuck didn't listen to him. The next day he flew into history!

The fastest speed anyone has travelled is 24,791mph (39,897km/h). This speed was reached by the crew of the spaceship *Apollo 10* on their return from space in 1969. It is a lot faster than any of the records set on Earth.

How fast can we go?

- in 1900 the Land Speed Record was 65.7mph (104km/h)
- in 2000 the Land Speed Record is 763mph (1227km/h).

What will it be in the year 2100? Or the year 3000?

One thing is sure – the speed freaks will never be satisfied!

CHANGING ETON

By the Same Authors
THE ETON BOOK OF THE RIVER

CHANGING

ETON

*A Survey of Conditions
based on the History of Eton since
the Royal Commission
of 1862-64*

BY
L. S. R. BYRNE & E. L. CHURCHILL

JONATHAN CAPE
THIRTY BEDFORD SQUARE
LONDON

FIRST PUBLISHED IN 1937

JONATHAN CAPE LTD., 30 BEDFORD SQUARE, LONDON
AND 91 WELLINGTON STREET WEST, TORONTO

PRINTED IN GREAT BRITAIN BY SPOTTISWOODE, BALLANTYNE
& CO. LTD. AND BOUND BY A. W. BAIN & CO. LTD.
PAPER MADE BY JOHN DICKINSON & CO. LTD.

CONTENTS

                                                          PAGE
PREFACE   I

CHAPTER I

A LARGE PREPARATORY SCHOOL BETWEEN 1870 AND 1880   3
A SMALL PREPARATORY SCHOOL AT ABOUT THE SAME DATE   12
A MEDIUM-SIZED PREPARATORY SCHOOL IN 1936   17
THE FALL IN EDUCATIONAL STANDARD OF BOYS NOW
    ENTERING PUBLIC SCHOOLS   21
HOME TEACHING   22
HOW TO BEGIN   24

ETON : *Introductory Note*   29
ABOLITION OF THE LOWER SCHOOL   30

CHAPTER II

ETON IN 1868, HOUSES, SCHOOLROOMS, MATHEMATICS,
    SCIENCE, FRENCH   31
POSITION OF THE HEADMASTER   33
POSITION OF NON-CLASSICAL MASTERS   36
THE ASSISTANT MASTERS, INCREASE IN NUMBER, LOSS OF
    THE PREPONDERANCE OF COLLEGERS AND KINGSMEN   41
DR. HORNBY'S BURDEN OF WORK   47

CHAPTER III

BITTER OPPOSITION TO DR. WARRE AND CONSEQUENT
    DIFFICULTY OF HIS POSITION   55
THE SCHOOL OFFICE, PRAEPOSTORS, TARDY BOOK, LEAVE   59
THE CALENDAR   66

v

CONTENTS

PAGE

TRIALS   70
WHAT DR. WARRE DID FOR ETON   71

CHAPTER IV

DR. LYTTELTON AND A PERIOD OF EXPERIMENT   73
ABOLITION OF COMPULSORY GREEK. ATTEMPT TO SUBSTI-
TUTE SCIENCE   75
UNSATISFACTORY NATURE OF THIS ARRANGEMENT AND
SUGGESTED REMEDY. DEVELOPMENT ARRESTED BY THE
WAR   76
DR. ALINGTON INTRODUCES THE INCLUSIVE FEE   83
HIS INFLUENCE   84

CHAPTER V

CURRICULUM OVERLOADED BY INTRUSION OF NEW SUBJECTS   87
NECESSITY OF RELIEF   91
EDUCATION SHOULD BE PRIMARILY LINGUISTIC AND LITERARY   91
FOR THE BEST BOYS LATIN AND GREEK PROBABLY STILL
ADVISABLE   92
FRENCH AND GERMAN A POSSIBLE ALTERNATIVE   92
DANGER OF ENGLISH AS A SEPARATE SCHOOL SUBJECT   93
HISTORY NOT IDEAL BECAUSE OF ITS INDEFINITENESS   96
GEOGRAPHY BEST TAUGHT IN COMBINATION WITH HISTORY   97
SCIENCE TEACHING FOR ALL BUT SPECIALISTS NEEDS DRASTIC
REVISION   98
SUGGESTION FOR THE INCORPORATION OF SO-CALLED EXTRA
SUBJECTS—DRAWING, MUSIC, WOOD AND METAL WORK,
BOXING, FENCING, PHYSICAL TRAINING   100

CHAPTER VI

CURRICULUM SHOULD BE SUITABLE FOR ORDINARY BOYS   111
THOROUGHNESS THE FIRST ESSENTIAL   112
DEMANDS OF UNIVERSITIES AN OBSTACLE TO PROGRESS   115
FAILURE OF LATIN DIVORCED FROM GREEK   117

CONTENTS

PAGE

PRESENT CONDITIONS RENDER LATIN, MATHEMATICS,
  FRENCH, HISTORY, INEVITABLE   120
ADVANTAGES OF GERMAN FOR THE ORDINARY BOY   124

CHAPTER VII

EVOLUTION OF THE BOARDING HOUSE   126
QUALITIES OF A SUCCESSFUL HOUSEMASTER   133
SEPARATE ROOMS   134
APPOINTMENT TO HOUSEMASTERSHIP   135
FINANCIAL PART PLAYED BY HOUSEMASTER   138
WHY COMPARATIVELY FEW ETON HOUSEMASTERS TAKE
  HEADMASTERSHIPS   139
HOUSE DISCIPLINE   139
LIBRARY   140
FAGGING   142
MEDICAL ARRANGEMENTS   144
THE SANATORIUM   144

CHAPTER VIII

PUPIL-ROOM AND SCHOOL   149
TUTORS AND HOUSES   153
ESSENTIAL SOUNDNESS OF TUTORIAL SYSTEM   155

CHAPTER IX

PROMOTION. TRIALS. EXTRA BOOKS   158
SCHOOL LEAVING CERTIFICATE. FIRST HUNDRED EXAM-
  INATION   167

CHAPTER X

COLLEGE CHAPEL. WALL PAINTINGS, WINDOWS, ORGAN,
  FLOOR, ALTAR AND ORNAMENTS, TAPESTRY, SIR
  GALAHAD   171
CHOIR AND SINGING. SERMONS   178

CONTENTS

	PAGE
CONFIRMATION	182
OVERCROWDING. CEMETERY CHAPEL. MUSIC ROOMS	182
LOWER CHAPEL. EXTENSION, PANELLING, WINDOWS, TAPESTRY, CHOIR	183
AUTHORITY OF PROVOST OVER BOTH CHAPELS	187

CHAPTER XI

| TOUR OF ETON. LISTS OF NEW BUILDINGS SINCE 1868. SUMMARY OF SAME | 189 |
| MATERIAL EQUIPMENT OF THE SCHOOL MOSTLY PROVIDED WITHIN LIVING MEMORY | 210 |

CHAPTER XII

SCHOOL DRESS A MATTER OF CONVENTION RATHER THAN OF RULE	212
GRADUAL DEVELOPMENT OF OUT OF SCHOOL COSTUMES	216
DECREASE IN RIGIDITY OF MANNERS AND DRESS	219
E.C.O.T.C. AND BOY SCOUTS	220

CHAPTER XIII

FOOTBALL ; GROUNDS ; ARRANGEMENT OF GAMES	225
CRICKET ; GROUNDS ; AGAR'S PLOUGH AND DUTCHMAN'S FARM ; ARRANGEMENT OF GAMES	229
FIVES ; BEAGLES ; ATHLETIC SPORTS ; RACKETS ; SQUASH RACKETS ; RUGBY FOOTBALL ; ASSOCIATION FOOTBALL ; FENCING ; BOXING ; GOLF ; LAWN TENNIS	236
SCHOOLBOY GAMES MENACED BY PUBLICITY	241

CHAPTER XIV

SCHOOL STORES ; BOOK POUND ; SCHOOL HALL	243
ETON SOCIETY OR POP	249
LIST OF OTHER SOCIETIES	250
BIRD SANCTUARY	251

CONTENTS

	PAGE
PICTURE GALLERY	252
MISSION	252

CHAPTER XV (EPILOGUE)

| WEAK POINTS OF MODERN EDUCATION. REMEDY | 254 |

APPENDIX	261
GLOSSARY	269
INDEX	275

LIST OF ILLUSTRATIONS

AERIAL VIEW OF ETON	*Frontispiece*
MAP I.—REPRODUCED FROM THE MAP IN THE ETON COLLEGE WORKS DEPARTMENT COMPILED BY MR. J. FISHER	*facing p.* 3
MAP II.—REPRODUCED BY PERMISSION FROM THE ORDNANCE SURVEY, 1932	,, 276

PREFACE

In this book an attempt is made to give some idea of education at Eton during the last half-century, what it was, its various phases of change and development, and what it now is. This is not a history of Eton, nor is it in the ordinary sense an educational work. The authors have had too much practical experience to propound any new theory or to claim the discovery of any royal road to perfection. What they have tried to do is this. They have set down, as objectively as possible, a description of the stages by which in their own school a simple system, which used to ignore more than half of each day in a boy's life and to devote the remainder exclusively to the acquisition of Latin and Greek, has gradually developed into the complex organism of to-day, which provides for almost every moment and rings the changes upon a bewildering multiplicity of subjects.

The authors themselves have known Eton as boys or masters for close on sixty years and have lived in daily association with many others whose experience went back beyond the middle of the last century. Their narrative therefore, where documentary evidence fails, is based on their own knowledge or on information received from those who took part in the events described.

Since 1860 many reminiscences of Eton have been

published, but no attempt seems to have been made hitherto to give a reasoned account of its educational development. The number of those whose recollections go back to the early years of the period is rapidly diminishing, and it is hoped that the following pages may help to perpetuate the knowledge of certain facts which must be put on record now if they are not to fall into oblivion.

ACKNOWLEDGMENTS

The authors wish to acknowledge their indebtedness to the late Provost, Dr. M. R. James, for valuable reminiscences both of his preparatory school and of Eton, given to them personally a short time before his death ; to Dr. Alington for permission to quote from *Things Ancient and Modern* ; to Mr. R. A. Austen-Leigh for many interesting suggestions that no one without his unrivalled knowledge of Eton records could have contributed ; to Mr. A. M. McNeile for drawing their attention to the *Memoirs of John Maude*, and to Mrs. Maude for permission to use them ; to Mr. J. Fisher, head of the College Works Department, for leave to reproduce his special map of Eton buildings ; and, finally, to two anonymous friends without whose help much of the chapter on preparatory schools would have been very difficult to write.

Eton College,
February 1937.

CHAPTER I

PREPARATORY SCHOOLS

The Old and the New

In some features Eton differs fundamentally from other public schools, but the main flow of the educational current is general throughout the country. It is therefore impossible to describe education at Eton without occasional reference to what is happening elsewhere, and above all in those preparatory schools where the vast majority of boys destined for a public school spend three or more of their most impressionable years.

One of the larger preparatory schools at the beginning of our period contained 130 boys, about 100 of whom lived in a fine red brick William and Mary building which stood in its own grounds close to Richmond Park. The remaining 30 boys were accommodated in the private houses of certain members of the staff. This school had a long history behind it, but not as a preparatory school in the modern sense. Before the year 1858, when it was taken over and transformed by an assistant master at Eton, formerly Scholar of Eton and King's, it had been, like most private schools of that time, a place where boys were received from the tenderest age up to 19. As will be seen shortly, some of the traditions

3

of this earlier type of school lingered into the seventies and eighties. The 130 boys were arranged in six classes under as many masters, each class being subdivided into α and β, one half preparing while the other was being heard. Every boy had a locker in which he kept books and papers. Four of these classes worked and had their lockers in one big schoolroom, the fifth class was in a sort of passage, while the first had a separate building all to itself with new and spotless lockers, in sharp contrast to the other schoolrooms with their dingy furniture inherited from former times. The school day was apportioned thus : At 7.30 all boys assembled in the big room, having previously received a Captain's biscuit. These biscuits were about 5 in. in diameter and nearly $\frac{3}{4}$ in. thick, so hard that even young teeth could scarcely break them, and so dry that few throats could swallow them. So they were mostly used as currency, six biscuits for three tea-sucks, the latter denoting cylinders of some kind of sugar through which tea could be sucked as through a straw. Then came brief prayers followed by about half an hour's school and breakfast. At nine the serious work of the morning began, in periods of one hour, and continued with little intermission till 12.30. The next half-hour was a period of wild scampering and screaming and was ended by somewhat sketchy washing of hands at a dreary row of cold-water basins placed just outside the diningroom. This was a preliminary to dinner, a turbulent ceremony lasting nearly an hour. The bread was

4

stale, the meat roughly cooked and still more roughly served, and the pudding often consisted of greasy suet with a little rhubarb or marmalade thrown in. Boys whose behaviour was too outrageous were sentenced by the Headmaster to a week's 'pig-table', a small serving-table in the middle of the room where they had to stand and scramble for what food could be got amid the jostling of the serving maids. The ordinary food was often so uneatable that boys brought in pieces of paper, wrapped up their dinner and hid it in the grounds or threw it down the drains except during one term when rats ate a large hole under one of the tables and waited in hordes for the food eagerly passed down to them. As boys had either to clear their plates or be punished, this simplified matters considerably. The writer must have been less squeamish than the average, for he remembers the offer of six pieces of butterscotch on condition of eating his neighbour's pudding. He accomplished the feat and has ever since respected that neighbour, who really did give him the butterscotch, all six pieces of it.

Games began immediately after dinner ; Rugby football in winter, cricket in summer. For football coats and waistcoats were removed, jerseys and a sort of woollen nightcap put on. For cricket matches the first eleven had a complete set of white flannels with a green elastic belt round their waists ; the others took off superfluous garments, retaining only what was indispensable. The Rugby goals were rather rotten and apt to fall suddenly with dire results. Except for the portion set apart for matches, the cricket ground, used for football also, was bumpy and the grass was often rather long. There was one boy high in the school, destined to win renown as Provost first of King's and then of Eton,[1] who more than once lost his spectacles in mid-pitch, whereupon the game was suspended and a couple of dozen small boys went down on all-fours to search. The feel of those spectacles triumphantly extracted from the coarse dry grass lives with one of them still. In a game such as this the batsman had one pad or none ; rarely one, perhaps never two gloves. As the wicket-keeper was likewise usually gloveless he required at least one longstop.

There was one fives court with a back wall and one side wall, both of them quite plain ; on wet days a sort of hockey was played with walking sticks in a small covered shed, already cumbered with play-boxes. A small and rather dark gymnasium floored with deep and dusty cocoanut fibre and fitted with a rope, parallel bars, a horizontal bar and a horse, provided occasional diversion in winter. A much-scarred drill-sergeant also sometimes taught a few elementary movements, but his chief occupation seemed to be 'Extra Drill', a gloomy but not altogether ineffective form of punishment which consisted in marching in fours for an hour round and round a gravel playground every day for a week or so. There was no provision for any other form of physical training.

[1] Dr. M. R. James, O.M.

At four o'clock on whole schooldays work was resumed and lasted till six. Then came tea, and after this a brief pause till preparation between seven and eight. There were half-holidays on Wednesday and Saturday, when there was no work after dinner except the evening preparation. In the summer, if any boy had won a scholarship or had been otherwise conspicuously virtuous the 'evening' was given, or in other words play was allowed in that most precious hour on a summer's day between seven and eight— or eight and nine, as it would now be called. Soon after eight bread and milk, the best meal in the day, was served, and bed followed, except on the weekly bath night, when boys were placed in rows in a set of shallow metal saucers and watched by the maids until they had scrubbed themselves thoroughly.

On Sunday mornings the whole school marched two and two into a neighbouring church, where it occupied most of one aisle. The afternoon was spent in walks, usually about Richmond Park, under the care of a harassed master. But to the evening of an otherwise dreary day a considerable number of boys looked forward with pleasure, for many of them were allowed into the Headmaster's drawing-room, where he read to them. As all that he did was interesting and on this one day of the week he ceased to be formidable, these evenings spent at what those who came to Eton learnt afterwards to call 'Sunday Private' stand out like gems.

The subjects taught to all boys were Latin, Greek, divinity, mathematics, history, geography and French.

B

The lower classes, those few which did no Greek, learnt writing under a master of inferior status. This writing was done in copy-books in characters apparently dating from the age of Cocker, and a favourite punishment was the setting of so many copies. The youthful hand was aching and cramped halfway down the first page, and sometimes the tale was six ! The bulk of the serious work consisted of Latin and Greek, both well taught throughout, and, towards the top of the school, with such accuracy as to leave an ineffaceable impression through life. In the middle of the school Latin verses were begun, and the chief Latin author was Cornelius Nepos. Cæsar was taken in the second class, Virgil in the first. Greek began with the Eton Sertum,[1] followed by Xenophon's Anabasis, Homer's Odyssey not being reached till the second class. A shortened Greek play was often not beyond the capacity of the first class. Divinity was taught by means of Maclear's Old and New Testament Histories. Mathematics (chiefly arithmetic varied by a little Euclid and towards the end some simple algebra) did not reach a very high standard. History was extracted from a textbook ; geography was inculcated by means of a series of maps done with a J pen and paint smeared on with the fingers ; French was very sketchy, though some was evidently learnt by the naturally proficient. If a boy was idle he was beaten by the Headmaster ; if he was among the first two or three in his class he

[1] A delightful collection of short extracts and humorous stories, now unluckily out of print.

8

was put on the Honour List, had a red cross against his name, was on half-holidays given sixpence and allowed to walk to Richmond with friends similarly privileged and buy what he liked. On one of these occasions the writer and two friends clubbed together to purchase one banana, an expensive fruit to them unknown. They did not think much of it.

Of the value of the classical teaching which was given at this school there is no doubt. It was clear, systematic, unhurried, and each individual realised that what he had learnt he was expected to know, and know accurately. Of course the masters varied in efficiency, but all were kept up to the mark by the knowledge that at any moment their class might be summoned to the Headmaster's study to have its lesson heard. These were occasions of terror, for not only was the Headmaster a formidable figure in himself, but he had a way of drawing in his breath, ejaculating as the victim shuffled and stammered, 'Don't bully me, sir !' and at the same time rattling the keys of a drawer in his table where a long ebony ruler reposed, ready to leap forth and do dire execution on the sluggard. A grammar in Latin which bore the name of 'Principia Latina' and was written by the Headmaster himself was learnt by heart and applied in every sort of way, so that its fundamental principles became to the learner part of his being. The assistant master who took the first class was an excellent teacher, but he was relieved when possible by the Headmaster, who, in addition, always set and corrected the weekly Latin prose, making the class learn and say to him his own fair copy, a fearful joy, but a joy none the less, for boys appreciate good teaching however stern. Nor was interest by any means confined to the classics. A completely un-expected lecture on Ogam inscriptions in Brittany lingers in the memory as an occasion when a whole class was glad to forgo its play hour rather than miss a word which fell from the Headmaster's lips.

Music was taught as an extra, and there was a school choir of some merit, no doubt chiefly due to an efficient master, but also perhaps in part to the tradition left by his predecessor, Sir Arthur Sullivan. This choir was rewarded for its efforts by a supple-mentary meal of cake and orange wine served on Sunday evenings at the Headmaster's big dining table. Beneath the table crawled unmusical friends of the singers, begging for scraps. To pass cake down into the dark was easy enough, and, though the orange wine was apt to lead to detection, it was hard for the privileged to resist the blandishments of their best friend on his marrowbones stroking their knees in silent supplication.

In winter it was impossible to keep even reasonably warm, chilblains were common and those not en-dowed with a lively circulation sat and worked with hands and feet icy. Summer brought almost equal suffering from thirst, apparently because water was thought bad for boys. Those who did not seem to the matron in charge to be overheated might get half a cup of water during a hot afternoon, but those who appeared panting and dishevelled were turned dry-lipped away. Luckily boys are inventive. Some managed to creep up to the dormitories and drink from jug and basin, all at some time or other resorted to the lavatory taps. These were turned off at the main immediately after dinner, but the taps were in rows, connected by a long, straight pipe, so a blower at one tap and a sucker a few taps along could extract the intervening fluid, and on any warm half-holiday afternoon boys could be found at work in couples till the precious store of water was exhausted.

Medical methods have advanced in sixty years, but it is hard not to believe that even for those days the treatment at this particular school was rough. When the writer first went there what was called 'ophthalmia'—perhaps some form of conjunctivitis— was raging. No steps at all were taken to deal with it, and, in his case at least, permanently impaired vision was the result. One thing the school authorities dreaded—vermin. Every week each boy had to bring his comb and present the top of his head to a matron, who made a perfunctory search, but no one ever heard of any captures. A boy who was suffering from some minor ailment unworthy of the comparative luxury of the sick cottage might be consigned to No. 19—the sick room—a small bare room at the top of the main building ; but it was disconcerting to be ejected suddenly, without cause assigned, and on return after a couple of hours to find the floor littered with tiny morsels of birch twig. These scraps were highly prized, for they were said to taste of brine and vinegar, and certainly rendered the occupant of No. 19 an object of envy.

So life was hard physically, and this, even if it did stunt the growth for a while, was good for the soul, and work, done under constant dread of the Headmaster's wrath, rod and birch, was always thorough and often interesting. For this his pupils owe him and his school an everlasting debt.

Of a somewhat different type were the small private schools of about thirty boys between nine and fourteen years of age. One of these was at Laleham, within three hundred yards of the Thames. Here the food was plain, but good and plentiful. School began at 7.30 A.M. It was preceded by a stout slice of bread and butter and some milk provided by the Headmaster's own cows. Breakfast was at 9 A.M., dinner at 2 P.M. and tea at 6 P.M. Hampers were allowed and clandestine visits were also paid to a sweet-shop in the village. Sometimes a boy would be lowered by a sheet after bedtime from a bedroom window in order to obtain supplies for a midnight banquet. On one such occasion the Headmaster became aware that something of the sort was going on and imagined that the means of egress were provided by a fine old pear tree which grew near the house. Characteristically enough he made no attempt to discover the culprits, but a day or two later, armed with an axe, he sallied forth and cut down the unoffending tree. Several boys, much puzzled, had gathered round to watch the operation, and when it was completed the Headmaster turned round with a grim smile and said, 'There, young gentlemen, I think that will stop your little games!' It was not till then that anyone had realised what was in his mind. A sheet was so much simpler!

Apart from the feeding the conditions of existence were somewhat primitive. Baths were limited to one a week—on Saturday night—and the only other forms of ablution consisted of a hasty wash in a basin of cold water about 7 A.M. and an occasional rinsing of the hands at a pump after football. On Thursdays even this perfunctory operation was impossible, as the outhouse in which the pump stood was then in possession of the laundry women who came in to do the household washing.

For games the boys went down to a field about a quarter of a mile away, took off their coats and waistcoats to play, put them on again after the game and went into school as they were. These games only took place once or twice a week. On other days every one had to amuse himself as best he could in a big playground, with no protection from cold or rain except a roof over one corner of a high brick wall, on the other side of which was the Headmaster's garden. Those who had finished their work had perforce to spend their time in this playground for the very good reason that there was nowhere else to go. If there were enough boys out of school a game of prisoner's base or something like it was usually started. But from the time when he went out across the playground into school before breakfast to the time when he went to bed no boy was allowed in the house. One outdoor closet with an open cesspool below it was the only sanitary accommodation.

In the summer the weekly bath was supplemented by occasional bathing. Once or twice a week the Headmaster would take nearly the whole of the school over the river to an excellent bathing-place, and many of the boys at the age of ten or twelve could swim across the Thames and back. Those who were not fairly proficient had to wait till the rest were ashore and were then taken into shallow water and taught.

The teaching, like everything else about the school, was of a rather Spartan character, but extremely good. Very rarely did a boy from Laleham fail to take Remove if he came on to Eton. The first school, as already mentioned, lasted from 7.30 to 8.45 A.M. After breakfast there was an interval of about half an hour ; then school again from 10 A.M. to dinner at two o'clock. There was no time-work ; a certain number of tasks, written or oral, had to be done by each boy. When they were finished to the Headmaster's satisfaction, that boy's work was over for the morning. Those who had failed to complete the amount set or had done it imperfectly went back into school directly after dinner and stayed there till they had produced what was required. At five o'clock work began again for all and, with a longish interval at six o'clock for tea, continued to eight o'clock, when the boys went to bed.

The teaching was in the hands of the Headmaster, one English assistant master and a Frenchman who came in every Thursday and took charge for the day. Any boy who believed that a Frenchman could not keep order was very rapidly and convincingly disabused of this idea at Laleham. The amount of work exacted on other days was pretty considerable, but Thursday was a day of terror. The lessons to be learnt and the exercises to be done kept everyone hard at it till after dinner, and the less fortunate went on till this wonderful man went away at four or five o'clock. Every bit of work had to be done again and again till it was right to the last accent. No sign of anger or threat of punishment ever escaped him ; but his face and figure might well have served a sculptor as a model for a statue of fate, and his methods were no whit less relentless.

The schoolroom was a long, narrow room with forms and desks along the side-walls and, running down the centre, a wooden table at which boys sat facing one another. Opening out of this room was a small annexe with desks on two sides. This held six or seven boys and was presided over by the assistant master. At the top of the central wooden table in the main schoolroom was the Headmaster's desk—an admirable strategic position, as from it he could without moving reach half a dozen boys or more with one of the two stout canes which with unfailing regularity he took out as soon as he came into school. But more often, when a lesson was being prepared, he walked up and down carrying a cane ; and woe to the unlucky boy who talked to his neighbour or appeared to be dreaming.

When the time came to construe or say by heart any lesson that had been learnt, the Headmaster sat down at his desk and three or four boys were called up to prove their knowledge. Those who failed to give satisfaction were told to hold out their hand, received a smart cut on it with the cane, took their book in that hand and held out the other. This continued till they had received two or three cuts on each hand, and then they were sent back to learn the lesson better. Under this system idleness did not flourish.

One admirable custom should be mentioned. At the end of each summer term two or three weeks were spent in learning between one and two hundred lines of Greek or Latin. This was called the Prize Task and took the place of all other work. When the time came for the examination all the boys had to be able not only to construe the passages set, but also to say them by heart and parse any word in them. The Prize Task for the year was learnt first in short lessons, then in longer ones, and finally as a whole. Those who did reasonably well in the examination were given a book, and very few ever failed to earn this reward, for failure might mean the loss of the first day of the holidays.

The system in force at this school would no doubt be considered brutal nowadays, but it had many merits. Thoroughness was the keynote of the place ; and the ignorance and want of application now displayed by many boys on their arrival at a public school would have been literally impossible to anyone who had been through this mill. In spite of his severity the boys with good reason respected and admired the Headmaster.

That preparatory schools should have changed somewhat in the course of sixty years was to be expected. The extent of the change may be gathered from the following brief account of an efficient school typical of the present time.

With eighty boys this school comes numerically about halfway between the two just mentioned; in general standard of work and in numbers of scholarships gained it is, so far as can be estimated, about their equal. The points of resemblance and of difference are therefore so interesting as to make it worth while to give in detail the time-table of a normal whole schoolday. Boys are called at 7.15, have breakfast at 7.45 and prayers at 8.40. Then follow:

Morning		*Afternoon*	
8.45	Latin.	1.40	Spelling, Prep., Drawing, etc.
9.30	French.		
10.15	Latin.	2.10	Drill and games.
10.45	Drill and out-door recreation.	4.15	Tea.
		4.45	Geography (3).
11.30	Mathematics.	5.30	Mathematics (3), Essay (1).
12.30	History (4). Science (2).		
1.0	Lunch.	6.15	Greek, Math., French or English.
		7.15	Supper.

The figures in brackets denote the number of days given to the subject each week.

At 7.45 there are prayers, then a free period till bedtime—8.30.

The above is a time-table for the two winter terms. In the summer the afternoon schools and games exchange places. In the winter terms Wednesday and Saturday are half-holidays, in the summer half-holidays are given as required for matches or other reasons.

On Sundays breakfast at 8.30 is followed by an hour's divinity teaching, and this in turn by eleven o'clock church. Half an hour is set apart for letters before lunch and another half-hour after it. The meals, with the exception of breakfast, are at the same times as on weekdays. Golf and lawn tennis may be played, or there may be a cinema show or a debate.

As each subject is taught simultaneously throughout the school, boys can be classified according to capacity, and the number of classes need not always be the same. In Latin and French there are 9 classes, in mathematics 7, in English 3, in Greek, which is taken by about twenty-five boys, also 3. Classes vary in number of boys from 16 to 7 and are frequently subdivided for teaching purposes.

A normal week's work contains some fifty periods, totalling in all about thirty-four hours. Of this time two subjects, Latin and mathematics, receive nearly sixteen hours between them, French and Greek (or alternatives as shown above) another ten, the remainder being shared by English, history, geography and science. The thirty-four hours represent practically the whole of the compulsory work, as even written exercises are done in school under direct supervision. There is no preparation out of school except occasionally in the case of candidates for some external examination.

Industry is encouraged by means of marks, place taking, rapid promotion, an occasional hour of work remitted for special merit, and prizes. There are two examinations each term, that at the end of the term, really a kind of glorified class-work, lasting ten days. About fifty boys take the Common Entrance Examination when it is in progress.

For punishment there is a system of marks, three bad marks a week entailing three-quarters of an hour's punishment drill and a silent walk of the same duration. If three marks are assigned too often, supper is curtailed and bed inflicted early. The last resort, the cane, is rarely used. On the other hand, a boy who for a fortnight gets no bad mark at all is let off one hour's work in school.

The three chief games, cricket, Rugby and Association football, are organised by masters and appear to be carefully taught, but apart from these the list of out-of-school occupations is long and varied. Drill, boxing and physical training are in the hands of a special instructor ; athletic sports are held in the summer to break the monotony of cricket ; less formal games are golf—a good links being situated just outside the school grounds—and lawn tennis, for which there are two grass courts and one hard. This latter game is played on Sundays and after supper. Besides these there are swimming, miniature rifle shooting, carpentry, skating when possible, gardening, said to be more of a pastime than a serious pursuit, singing, dancing, theatricals, a cinema, and the various collection manias which attack all boys in turn, such as butterflies and stamps. All these are directly encouraged, so that there is a chance of development for almost every taste.

The prominence attained by outdoor sports is reflected in costume. Sixty years ago a small boy had a suit of best clothes for Sundays consisting usually of light trousers, Eton jacket, waistcoat and collar, topped by a bowler hat; for weekdays, an ordinary suit of almost any pattern used for games and school alike. In the water he had no clothes at all. Quite apart from what he wears in school the small boy now has appropriate outfits for cricket, athletic sports, drill, swimming, and two kinds of football. The gain in cleanliness, health and self-respect is great, but so is the increase in cost.

Boys thus closely occupied and supervised during most of their waking hours might be expected to develop little sense of responsibility, but an attempt has been made to deal with this difficulty by the institution of prefects, who are expected to assist the master on duty, and of captains of dormitories, who are authorised to inflict bad marks for misbehaviour. This latter deterrent is said to be so efficient that little trouble is caused except by new boys.

The Headmaster and his family live among the boys, without trying to reserve any part of the house for private use.

The typical preparatory school of the present date is thus a well-knit but complicated organisation making heavy demands on all who run it, and occupying almost every moment of a boy's life during term-time. This is true despite the not infrequent holidays, for it will be found that a holiday, though given as a reward, is usually devoted to some definite object —a match or an expedition. Boys who have passed through such a school come to Eton better mannered, cleaner, healthier and perhaps happier than their predecessors, but they have lost something in rude independence, in realisation that they will not always be protected from the consequences of their own folly, and, last, but perhaps most important, their mental outlook, though it may be broader, is less clear. For the better boys this may not matter much in the long run. They always manage somehow to disentangle themselves ; but the average, and still more the slow, may never recover from the rush and confusion of a multitude of subjects all clamouring for simultaneous attention. Again, just as with good boys, so in a good school, the difficulty is often surmounted, but in the weaker schools, as among the weaker boys, diffusion of aim has caused loss in efficiency compared with the single-hearted devotion to grammar, text and dictionary of former days. Consequently in the ordinary stock subjects the average standard of candidates for admission to Eton is lower than used to be the case. Whether the loss has been compensated for in other respects it is hard to say.

It has to be remembered, however, that the preparatory schoolmaster of fifty or sixty years ago had certain great advantages over his modern counterpart. The boys sent to him were sent to him, first and foremost, in order that they might learn Latin and Greek, all other subjects being of quite secondary importance. They came to him already thoroughly grounded at any rate in Latin and probably in arithmetic. It was nothing very unusual for a boy to arrive at his preparatory school knowing a great portion of the Latin Primer perfectly. Greek could therefore be started at once, and after two years several boys were able to learn fifteen or sixteen lines at a time of Homer's Iliad with no help but a text and a dictionary ; and often these lines had to be said by heart after they had been construed. This meant that the teaching given at home—narrow though it was, and useless as much of the knowledge acquired would appear to modern ideas—had given these boys the capacity for sitting down to a difficult task unaided, and wrestling with it till it was mastered. The preparatory schoolmaster of to-day probably never finds a single boy who has been drilled into this habit before his arrival at school.

This falling off in the power of application is partly the result of the wider range of subjects now insisted on, partly of the great decrease in the use of the rod, for which no satisfactory substitute has been found, and partly of the postponement of all serious teaching owing to the idea, common to mothers and the medical profession, that there is a danger of over-

working the child's mind. Such a danger there may
be in the case of a few brilliant, highly strung boys ;
but the difficulty with the vast majority is to make
them use their minds at all ; and, provided that they
are not given unduly long hours, they are secured
by nature against any risk of strain. It is precisely
among boys of this kind that the standard has fallen
so seriously. Even after they have left home their
rate of progress is apt to be slower than in former
days. For it is safe to assume that, if the older schools
suffered from some excess of harshness in their
methods, and from a certain narrowness of scope, the
newer ones often go to the opposite extreme in both
respects. This is hardly surprising. On the one
hand the private schoolmaster knows that many
parents imagine that, if only a beginning is made
with enough subjects, the dullest boy will find something to interest him ; on the other the maternal
instinct naturally makes it impossible for most
mothers to believe that their own little boy is inclined
to be lazy and needs a certain amount of severity to
make him apply himself to tasks that in themselves
do not appeal to him. Yet such tasks must of
necessity form the bulk of his work for a considerable
period ; for, as the Germans say, *aller Anfang ist
schwer*—all first steps are difficult.

To such parental views no headmaster of a preparatory school can afford to be indifferent. The
competition between these schools is now so great,
and the expense of running them is so much increased by modern demands, that any diminution of

numbers entails a financial loss which makes it difficult to resist the pressure of public opinion ; and in this case public opinion is apt to mean the opinion of the majority of mothers. There is no doubt that a considerable amount of regular instruction should be given to nearly all children from the age of five onwards, and that those whose education is not begun till two or three years later are being unjustifiably sacrificed to fears of some purely imaginary evil consequences that may attend the exercise of a brain that nature meant to be used.

What this regular instruction should comprise is a question to which widely different answers have been given. It must be said at the outset that no rules can be laid down for exceptionally gifted parents who have the originality to devise their own methods for their children's education and the time and energy to apply them in person. The same is true of all those teachers who have sprung upon the world some new system to which they ascribe the supremely successful results in reality attributable to their own individuality and genius. But methods of an unusual kind in the hands of men and women of ordinary capacity lose their efficacy and often serve to bewilder rather than enlighten an immature mind. There is, however, a middle path—a compromise between the extreme rigidity of fifty years ago and the excessive flexibility of ultra-modern theories.

But before any suggestions are made for a scheme of general application it may be of interest to give a brief account of what is being done at the present moment in the case of a particular boy. It may be premised that Peter, as he shall be called, is both physically and mentally above rather than below the average, and the same may be said of his parents. That this should be so is almost inevitable owing to the difficulty of getting accurate information from any but the more clear-headed type of parent.

Peter, writes his mother,

'went to the Montessori class at the age of $5\frac{1}{2}$, where he learnt childish values in weights and measures, elementary arithmetic, geography, history, reading, writing, and a certain amount of French. At seven he could read and write really well ; knew his twelve times tables, dodging inclusive ; now at the age of eight he knows the four Rules of Arithmetic in an elementary form, plus money sums of most kinds and mental arithmetic ; geography, very good maps, knows quite fairly certainly all countries and capitals of the world, oceans, big canals, a certain amount about Africa, including big rivers and mountains, and an odd smattering of general knowledge of most countries. History, taught at school, a fair amount of Greek, Roman and Ancient British, also stone and bronze age, plus knowledge of a fair amount of English heroes at sea and on land, and a slight knowledge of kings, but no dates for kings or events, perhaps 1066, no more ! ! Compositions and elementary English grammar and elocution of a sort. Good spelling and dictation. Nature study, plants and animals. Scripture quite varied. Reading out loud at the moment Stories of the North. French he seems to have forgotten, because at the moment he is not learning it, but I think it is safely there. It seems to me that Peter's strong point—in fact most boys' —is his general knowledge on almost every conceivable thing. He lives on it. But whether it is too varied and without actual depth to be good I do not know.'

What is said above about geography may be to some extent discounted, as home conditions are in Peter's case exceptionally calculated to make this subject a matter of everyday interest. The letter continues with an account of his boxing, football and so on, which need not be set down in full ; but the concluding criticism cannot be omitted. Summing up the situation the writer suggests that in spite of its wide range Peter's education may have been not wholly satisfactory,

> 'as he lacks concentration for the things he does not like, and that is where to my mind modern education fails. They cannot teach concentration. He adores history, geography, nature study, reading, but mathematics he dislikes, and so does not do too well.'

In these last sentences the writer has put her finger on the weak spot of modern teaching, not only in the early stages, but throughout. If the teaching of fifty years ago erred on the side of disregard for a boy's tastes, that of to-day errs more seriously in paying overmuch attention to them. No education is worth having that does not teach the lesson of concentration on any task required, however unattractive. It should be remembered that the ultimate test of a properly trained intelligence is its capacity to apply itself at will to whatever work confronts it and to persevere with that work till it is done. These lessons, if not learnt early, will be learnt, if at all, with pain and grief in later life. It is little less than criminal insanity to waste the impressionable years of early childhood in groping vaguely about to discover imaginary tastes in a mind as yet incapable of forming any judgment on any matter, however simple, and swayed by likes and dislikes varying from moment to moment with incalculable fickleness.

It is now time to return from this digression to the question of the subjects to be taught before the preparatory school age and of the order in which they are to be taken. Exact time limits cannot be assigned to any plan for the first steps in a child's education. The rate at which knowledge is acquired will naturally vary according to the innate capacity and the environment of the individual. But the subjects to be taught and the order in which they should be taken can be fairly accurately defined. Reading, writing and spelling should come first, followed, as soon as the symbols can be recognised, by the four chief rules of arithmetic. In the next stage, which should normally be reached in about two years, the teaching of arithmetic should be carried as much further as personal aptitude renders possible ; a start should be made with the elements of Latin ; and, if a little conversational French is available, so much the better.

27

In English, once the meaning of the Parts of Speech
has been grasped, emphasis must be laid on the
structure of the ordinary sentence. It must be
pointed out that every clause is built up round a
verb ; that sentences are divided into simple and
compound—the former containing one verb, the
latter two or more ; that each clause may contain
besides the verb three other components, the subject
and anything that qualifies it, the object with the
same possible additions, and an adverb or adverbial
expression ; and that in a compound sentence the
clauses are joined together by certain links, the
words which can perform this conjunctive function
falling into three classes which are called, respectively,
conjunctions, relatives and interrogatives. It will be
found that the analysis of an English sentence on
these lines will provide a sound basis later on for the
study of Latin and other languages. It is not the
purpose of this book to give a detailed introduction
to English grammar, but this subject has for many
years been so gravely neglected throughout the whole
country, that it has seemed necessary to emphasise
its importance and to give a brief outline of the way
in which it should be approached.

ETON

Introductory Note

The following table shows the names used for the different parts of the school since 1850. Sixth Form is the highest, First (subsequently Third) Form the lowest. For further information see Chapter IX; for terms peculiar to Eton see Glossary (p. 269).

Up to 1860	*From 1884*	
UPPER SCHOOL	UPPER BOYS	
Sixth Form	Sixth Form	
Fifth Form	First Hundred	A
Upper Division	Fifth Form	
Middle Division	Upper Division	B
Lower Division	Middle Division	C
Remove	Lower Division	D
Fourth Form		
LOWER SCHOOL	LOWER BOYS	
Third Form	Remove	E
Upper Greek	Fourth Form	F
Lower Greek	Third Form	F
Sense		
Nonsense		
Second Form		
First Form		

The subdivisions of Third Form had disappeared by 1862 ; and about the time of Mr. J. W. Hawtrey's retirement in 1869 First and Second Form were abolished, after which the terms Upper and Lower School ceased to have any real meaning. Previously Lower School had been a kind of preparatory school with a separate organisation. The names upper and lower boys survived, though in a rather different sense. Fourth Form and Third Form were put under the control of the Lower Master, and counted as lower boys. Sixth Form, First Hundred (when instituted) and Fifth Form were all upper boys. Remove was not put under the Lower Master till 1905, though the boys in it counted as lower boys for the purpose of games, fagging and the like.

Some perplexity may well be caused by the two-fold use of the word 'remove'. The Upper, Middle and Lower Divisions of Fifth Form have three sub-divisions apiece, and these subdivisions are called removes. The block known as Remove is similarly subdivided. Boys normally spend one Half in each of these removes. Fourth Form is divided into Upper, Middle and Lower Fourth.

CHAPTER II

REFORM AT ETON

Dr. Hornby and his times

The previous chapter has dealt with the laying of the foundations on which public schools have to build. The next few chapters will be devoted to an attempt to describe the continuation of the educational structure and the evolution of the system now in existence at the school with which this book is mainly concerned, as being to a large extent typical of what has happened in the majority of other public schools.

At Eton, as in England generally, change is gradual, almost imperceptible, but occasionally a step is taken big enough or conspicuous enough to attract attention. Press and public, unaware that what is happening is nothing but the registration or recognition of development already well advanced, claim all the credit for the reform.

The appointment in 1868 of Dr. Hornby, an Oppidan and an Oxford man, was a step of this kind. It marked a stage in the slow disappearance of the age-long tradition that Collegers and Kingsmen in Holy Orders were alone qualified to teach Eton boys, and that the only subject worthy of their notice was classics.

Before Dr. Hornby's reforms are considered, something must be said of the conditions which he found prevailing at Eton on his return as Headmaster.

Of houses in 1868 there were twenty-eight, varying in size from about half a dozen boys to fifty ; nine of them ranked as dames' houses, over which the Head-master had till a short time before had no jurisdiction as to succession or numbers. The tutors', or classical masters' houses as they would now be called, were already under some sort of control.

Schoolroom accommodation had recently been greatly improved by the erection in 1863 of the New Schools, the block of rooms grouped round the Cannon Yard, numbered 1 to 15. The older school-rooms were poor. Six or seven, described by a contemporary as 'disgracefully primitive and uncom-fortable',[1] were in School Yard ; a dreary row of half a dozen were on the site of part of the present Queen's Schools, where also was a strange edifice called from its shape the Rotunda, used for music, lectures and science. As both boys and masters were at the time rapidly increasing in numbers, it is difficult to say what would have happened but for pupil-rooms, which then, as now, when other accom-modation ran short, had to be used for school. The mathematical schools to the north of the New Schools, numbered 16 to 31, did not come into use till 1877.

As regards work, emphasis was slowly shifting from pupil-room to school, and, perhaps in consequence, from tutor to house. Until well past the middle of

---

[1] *Memoirs of John Maude* (at Eton, 1860–1869), privately printed 1936.

the century most of the serious work must have been done in pupil-room,[1] since the school divisions contained some forty-five boys apiece, and the number of school periods in a normal week at that time never exceeded eighteen. Under Dr. Hornby this figure became twenty-one, and the size of the divisions was diminished by an increase of 25 per cent. in the number of masters. Under Dr. Hornby also the dames' houses in the old sense were disappearing, for thenceforward none but regular masters of the school might receive boys. Thus the Headmaster gained control of succession to houses, and, within limits laid down by the College, of the numbers in them. The change was sealed in 1882, when the three columns in the School List which had hitherto read :

'Name   Tutor   House'

became, 'Name   House Tutor   Classical Tutor' ;

but its significance was not realised at the time, and it hardly became definitely established until after the disappearance of the last and greatest of dames' houses in 1906.

Lastly, the Headmaster, emerging from his old position as chief teacher, absorbed in the routine of his own division, and only sallying forth occasionally as judge or executioner, began to take some part in general supervision. Nevertheless this particular Headmaster's time was still taken up in teaching, for an account of him furnished by a member of his

---

[1] See Chapter VIII, p. 149.

Sixth Form in the seventies describes him with gratitude as a brilliant and accomplished exponent of scholarship and makes no mention of any other activity. He certainly worked hard, so hard that he was usually inaccessible to boys and masters alike, and interviews had to be arranged by appointment. The surprise and anger were therefore great in the rare crises when—as in the dismissal of Oscar Browning for insubordination—he played the part which nowadays would be deemed to belong to the ordinary functions of a Headmaster.

Such were the conditions at the time of Dr. Hornby's appointment. He took office on the understanding that mathematics, science and French were thenceforward to be taught to every boy during his school career.

By 1868 mathematics were already pretty firmly established, and had been so for longer than is generally supposed. In the School Lists for Election 1845 and 1847 and Easter 1849 there appear, as an appendix, lists of 'The Mathematical School', which, besides showing that about two-thirds of the boys learnt mathematics, prove that the classical assistant masters were far from hostile to the subject. 'Since the year 1837', says the preface to these lists, 'the Assistant Masters have annually given a prize of Books, of the value of Ten Guineas, to the most proficient in the Study of Mathematics.'

'The Mathematical Master gives a second prize of the value of Four Guineas.'

'The Assistant Masters have also given a junior

Prize, value Two Guineas, to the best Arithmetician among the Lower Boys.'

In 1847 and 1849 many names are marked with the mysterious symbol μ, which a footnote explains as meaning μύσται—the Greek term for those initiated in certain mysteries. What were the particular mysteries into which they were initiated as contrasted with those mathematicians who had not earned this symbol is nowhere explained.

In the 1847 list it is noted that 'George Tomline Esq. has made over to the College in trust the yearly Interest of £1000 Stock to be given annually to the best Proficient among the Scholars of the Mathematical Master'; and further that in consequence of this 'the Assistant Masters have decided to give Two Prizes, of the value of Eight and Four Guineas, to the Second and Third in order of Proficiency.' At the same time two prizes, of two guineas and one guinea, were given by the assistant masters, and one prize of two guineas by the Lower Master, to the best and second best of the lower boys.

In 1851 mathematics were incorporated in the regular work of the school. For some time, however, an extra charge of four guineas a year was made in order to provide funds for the salaries of the masters who taught them. The report of the Public Schools Commission reveals how scanty the remuneration was. It was drawn from four sources—the proceeds of this extra charge, fees for private tuition, profits on boarders and a sum of about £120 paid by the Headmaster to provide a seventh mathematical

master. Of the first of these just over half went to
Mr. Stephen Hawtrey, the head of the mathematical
school. In 1860 the amount available for his
assistants was only £2,786 19s.—under £400 a year
each. When it is remembered that nearly £1,400
of this came from fees for private tuition and boarding
fees, and that in 1862 one master had forty private
pupils out of about a hundred available, it is clear
that some must have been trying to live on a little
over £200 a year, though the Commissioners state
that 'we are informed that an Assistant Master with
a family can hardly live at Eton under £800 a year'.
It is therefore not surprising that the terms offered
did not attract the most eligible of the then small
number of men suitable for the position.

Between 1851 and the appointment of the Public
Schools Commission it seems to have been laid down
that a certain knowledge of mathematics was necessary for promotion in the school. Mr. Stephen
Hawtrey stated in his evidence that boys were not
allowed 'to go into Lower Greek', *i.e.* the second
division of the Lower School, till they knew 'the first
four rules of Arithmetic', and that they could not be
admitted to Fifth Form without 'Fractions, Decimals,
Rule of Three and Interest'.

In spite of the comparatively satisfactory status of
the subject, those who taught mathematics were still
in a position of inferiority compared to classical
masters. Up to 1853, in which year Dr. Hodgson
died and was succeeded as Provost by Dr. Hawtrey,
they were not allowed to wear academical costume.

Under Dr. Goodford this restriction was removed and some of them were allowed to hold boarding houses ; but even in 1862 they were still regarded as 'Domines'—the name given to men who held houses on the same terms as 'Dames'—and had no share in maintaining the discipline of the school. Nor were they allowed to hold any of the larger houses. Mr. Edward Hale tells the Commissioners that if during the Windsor Fair 'I walk down and see any of the boys, they would not get out of my way or leave the Fair if I told them to go to Eton. They would not, however, allow a classical assistant master to see them, and, if he did, they would get out of the Fair at once.' As the same witness observes, this was rather ludicrous in view of the fact that two of the mathematical masters treated with so little consideration were Fellows of Trinity College, Cambridge.

Dr. Hornby removed, as far as was then possible, all distinctions between classical and other masters. Further, besides retaining the three weekly periods already given to mathematics, he assigned two to French from the top of Upper Division downwards, and two to science in certain blocks. But the risk was great, as for many years adequate teaching power was unobtainable. As already shown, in mathematics, taught at the Universities and with a certain established tradition, this difficulty was overcome sooner than in other new subjects. But modern languages maintained a precarious existence for more than a generation without making any deep impression on the work, and the struggle of science lasted longer still, and, until Dr. Alington became Headmaster, the majority of boys can hardly be said to have taken it seriously. It must, however, be remembered that in one sense French and science are not recent importations. As long ago as 1766 there were two French masters attached to the school—M. Lemoine and M. Antoine Pyron du Martre, who took the name of Anthony Porny, and founded the Porny school ; while another Frenchman, M. Duclos, published in 1804 *An Introduction to the French Tongue for the use of Eton School*. And in 1847 Mr. Edward Solly, F.R.S., was invited to Eton to give a course of 'Experimental Lectures in Chemistry and Natural Philosophy', and he reports that 'I have carefully looked over the Examination Papers, and have much pleasure in saying that they are very far better than I expected. Twenty-four are decidedly good.' He then gives the names of the four best in order of merit and of the next seven in alphabetical order, and concludes : 'These have all answered the questions correctly, and in such a manner as to evince considerable knowledge of the subject.'

In more recent times it may be noted that in 1872 French was made compulsory in the entrance examination, and that in the Lent Half of 1874 there were 28 boys in First Hundred and 236 in Upper and Middle Division doing science for two hours a week.

The introduction of mathematics, French and science was therefore by no means sudden, and for more than sixty years they have been taught continuously. Their failure to establish themselves after so many years' trial was attributed by those interested in an education primarily or exclusively classical to the inherent inferiority of the subjects. They forgot that in its early stages a new branch of knowledge requires teachers not below but above the average, and that these can only be produced after a considerable lapse of time. No doubt this may be an argument against changes of any kind unless they are demonstrably indispensable ; it is certainly a warning against hasty action or change for the sake of change.

To find men with good technical proficiency in a new subject is not necessarily impossible ; in fact at Eton some of the pioneers in mathematics, science and the rest were at least as distinguished intellectually as any of their successors ; but unhappily, with few exceptions, they lacked all the other qualities which go to make an efficient schoolmaster.

Dr. Hornby had begun to face the necessity of admitting to the general curriculum subjects other than Latin and Greek. But during his reign these two subjects were still the staple of school work and the only ones that boys took seriously. Despite the occupation of one-third of his time in school with modern subjects, the average boy in Dr. Hornby's day felt sure, not only that classics were the only thing that really mattered, but that, when on Wednesdays his weekly copy of verses was shown up, the bulk of what that week required of him was over.

He could protest volubly against the sums in his Extra Work being marked wrong, he could write pages and pages of Science Abstract in the certainty that they would be marked by weight, and he could smuggle his Greek iambics into French school and do them there. Then, when out of school he found one classical master coaching the Eight, another looking after the Eleven, a third commanding the Corps and a fourth presiding over Passing, he knew, not only that classics were the only subject of importance in school, but that they alone brought proficiency outside.

The changes made by Dr. Hornby in fulfilling the conditions of his appointment brought up a fresh set of problems. Diversity of subjects involved an increase in the numbers of the staff and a radical change in their capacities. Control was rendered more difficult by the increase of numbers, and organisation by the diversity of subjects. The nature of these problems and the steps taken to solve them may now be considered in greater detail.

First there was the question of the teaching staff.

In 1841 there were sixteen masters, all of them clergymen, all but one old Collegers, all but two from King's. The only non-Etonian taught mathematics. The proportion of masters to boys was roughly 1 : 45.

By 1868 the number had risen to thirty-one, of whom nineteen were in Orders, eighteen old Collegers from King's, and seven taught either mathematics

or science. The proportion of masters to boys was
1 : 28.

In 1884, of forty-four masters fifteen were in Orders,
fifteen old Collegers from King's, thirteen taught
mathematics or science and three French. The proportion of masters to boys had fallen to 1 : 20.

Ten years later (1894) the number of masters
was fifty-six, thirteen of them in Orders, thirteen
old Collegers from King's, twenty-one taught non-
classical subjects. Masters stood to boys in the
proportion of 1 : 18.

The process has continued steadily ever since until
in the year of writing (1936) there are eighty-four
masters, or one to fourteen boys ; the number of
Kingsmen has shrunk still further in proportion to the
total ; of the forty-one Old Etonians nearly half are
Oppidans ; only thirty-nine teach any classics at
all ; only two are in Orders. Nearly all have a
University degree, though a few, and these by no
means the least efficient, depend on other qualifications.

The change may be seen more clearly in the following table, which gives the figures at the beginning
of the headmasterships of Drs. Hawtrey, Hornby,
Warre and Lyttelton, and at the present time.

Year	Boys	Masters	Ratio	Eton-King's	In Orders	Class.	Math.	Mod. Lang.	Sci.	Hist.	Drawing
1841	716	16	1 : 45	14	16	15	1	—	—	—	—
1868	866	31	1 : 28	18	19	24	6	—	1	—	—
1884	894	44	1 : 20	15	15	28	9	3	4	—	—
1905	1021	61	1 : 17	15	7	32	14	9	4	1	1
1936	1158	84	1 : 14	12	2	39	16	14	9	4	2

'Extra masters'—those whose subjects are not included in the regular time-tables—do not appear in this list.

To return again for a moment to 1841. The Headmaster at that time presided over little more than a dozen men, all of the same cloth as himself, all not only Etonians, but Collegers, who had spent their whole boyhood together, all from the same University and almost all from the same college in that University, men whom he must have known from childhood. Nor was this the end of the influence of Eton and King's, for the Provost and Fellows who had selected the Headmaster, and to whom he was responsible, were drawn exclusively from the same sources. The curriculum he had to administer was uniform throughout the school and traditional, as were likewise most of the books used.

Secondly, the Headmaster's control over all school institutions had to be rendered effective. In 1841, although there were already some tutors' houses, the majority of the boarding houses, seventeen to be exact, were dames', and over them the Headmaster had but slight authority. Chapel, still called Church, was then, as now, in the hands of the Provost, and its services were carried on with but little regard to the school, all sermons, for instance, being preached as of right by the Fellows, a custom which was to last for another forty years.[1] The scope of the Headmaster was therefore limited. His first duty was to teach the highest division in the school ; his second

[1] See Chapter X, pp. 180–2.

to call Absence, maintain discipline and deal with offenders whose names were sent to him ; his third, the selection of his assistants, was almost automatic, so narrow was the field of recruitment. Thus it was in teaching the highest division in the school that the Headmaster spent most of his time, and this was almost the only opportunity afforded him of showing his capacity.

When Dr. Hornby was appointed in 1868 the situation had already undergone considerable change. That the new Headmaster himself was an Oppidan from Balliol and Brasenose has already been mentioned, as also that the number of assistant masters was almost double what it had been a quarter of a century earlier, and that thirteen of them were not from King's and twelve were laymen.

But this was not the only cause which altered the relations of the Headmaster to his work. In the first place the dames' houses, formerly seventeen, were at the beginning of the new reign only seven in number, and at the end only one remained ; and with every additional house taken over by one of his own assistants the influence of the Headmaster was increased. How far this was so may be shown by two instances. One was a case of a house where proper order was not maintained. The house was broken up and the master relegated to teaching only. The other was that of a master who exceeded the limit of numbers ordained for his house. He was dismissed ; and there is little doubt that discipline gained greatly thereby. There had been some danger of the headmastership becoming a feudal suzerainty, each housemaster being lord of his own castle, but Dr. Hornby's lesson went home and has not needed repetition ; and Eton owes him much for his restoration of discipline among masters and boys.

The third problem that required solution had been caused by the disappearance of uniformity in the previous training of the teaching personnel and in the nature of the subjects taught. It could no longer be assumed with confidence that every master was equally capable of teaching all that was needed in any part of the school, for already some masters specialised in mathematics or science, and this was merely a foretaste of what was to follow. Thus, simultaneously, the narrow limitations formerly imposed by custom on the choice of masters disappeared, and the increase in the number of subjects taught called for men whose education had not been on the old, stereotyped lines. In this way the Headmaster's task in selecting a staff which should be capable of dealing adequately in school with a varied curriculum, and should also, individually, be of the type required to make efficient housemasters, was rendered infinitely harder. The arrangement of the work and the distribution of school hours among the different subjects also demanded more attention, and the doubling of the staff added greatly to the labour of organisation.

Dr. Hornby's work as Headmaster affected the life of the school in so many directions that there is a danger that an account that deals with the development of Eton under various headings may fail to do justice to what he accomplished. The following summary of the changes which he introduced will, perhaps, serve to make the situation clear.

For the old Chapel service from 3 to 4 on half and whole holiday afternoons he substituted the short daily morning service that still exists.

He provided better Chapel accommodation for lower boys.

He put mathematics, French and science on a regular footing.

He doubled the number of schoolrooms available.

He abolished the junior school.

He confined the appointment to houses to regular masters of the school and abolished, in this respect, the distinction between classical and non-classical men.

He thereby established control over the succession to houses, and made the limitation of numbers in them a reality.

He added a school at 9.45 on half-holiday mornings.

He allowed the tutor to set a piece of Latin prose instead of Verses in A and B, and abolished the pupil-room theme in favour of Latin prose done in school.

He was responsible for the introduction of the larger school list with columns giving the names of each boy's tutor and house.

During his headmastership the number of the staff was increased from 31 to 44.

Nevertheless Dr. Hornby came to Eton imbued with the old tradition that the chief duty incumbent on the Headmaster was to undertake unaided the entire work of his own division of thirty-two of the best boys in the school. How nobly he accomplished this task is proved by the enthusiasm and gratitude with which distinguished scholars write to this day of the teaching received from him. But it could only be done at a cost. He had to deny himself to all and sundry during many days in each week, and even to take refuge from chance interruptions in his cottage at Black Potts. To see him without special appointment was difficult. In fact, towards the end of his reign masters, boys and Old Etonians learnt to regret that glimpses of him came few and far between.

In spite of these difficulties he adhered rigidly to the programme set him by tradition. One of the most fatuous items in this programme was the system under which the calling of Sixth and Fifth Form Absence devolved on the Headmaster alone. This meant that never less than three and sometimes as many as nine times in the week he had to call over about six hundred boys, an operation which occupied twenty-five minutes or more. Nor was this all. No organisation existed for the production of the list of names, which had to be written out either by the Headmaster himself, or, as popularly believed, by his butler ; though even in the latter case he must himself have done the preliminary work. The full tale of Absences was occasionally diminished by a 'Call'[1] ; but still the waste of time was enormous.

The result of all this was that, while he remained Headmaster, Dr. Hornby was greatly overworked and had no opportunity of revealing to the mass of the school his more human side, or of showing the interest which anybody with his athletic record—he played in the Eton cricket eleven as a boy, rowed for Oxford in 1849, '50 and '51, and, at Henley, was in the Oxford crew that won the Grand in the two latter years, while in 1850 he won the Stewards and the Goblets in addition—was bound to feel in their rowing and cricket. A marked change took place when he became Provost in 1884, and from that date onwards there was no more constant attendant at the practice of the Eight and the cricket matches in Upper Club. His unremitting labour has, however, had its reward, for in certain externals at least, such as the daily morning Chapel and the general lay-out of school hours and Absences, his plan remains to the present day.

Dr. Hornby had been appointed by the Provost and the old Fellows of the College in order that he should carry out the reforms judged to be necessary by the Parliamentary Commission. How faithfully he did his work has just been shown. The least he

---

[1] A 'Call' meant that there was no Absence. The original phrase was 'Praepostor's Call', implying that in the absence of the Headmaster it was the duty of the Praepostor (see p. 60) to call the names, though it is doubtful if he ever did so. In any case the result is paradoxical, as Absence means a function at which all boys must be present, whereas a 'Call' means that no names are called.

had the right to expect was the loyal support of the new Governing Body installed by that same Commission. But this he was very far from receiving, as will appear from what follows.

On September 26, 1873, a communication, signed, not by the Provost but by the clerk, a paid official, and headed 'By direction of the Governing Body', was sent to the Headmaster. It runs :

ETON COLLEGE,
26th September, 1873.

Reverend Sir,

The new Governing Body of Eton College have directed me to inform you that, having had under their consideration at a meeting held yesterday, a Circular dated the [ ] day of July, 1873, which has been sent by most of the holders of Boarding Houses to the Parents of the Boys in their Houses, and purporting to be issued with your approbation ; and having also received a Letter from you, dated the 24th instant, in which it is stated that the Circular was sent with your knowledge and consent, though you did not like the way in which it was worded ; they consider it essential for the good government of the School that the facts of the case, and the mode of dealing with it, should be clearly understood.

The facts of the case are—

Firstly.—Some months after regulations had been made with the concurrence of the Special Commissioners, fixing the charge for Board and Lodging, the Governing Body, after considering a Memorial of the Assistant Masters, in which they suggested that an additional sum of £11 per annum for each boy should be allowed for maintenance, agreed to recommend to the Special Commissioners that an increased charge for maintenance, from £99 to £105 per annum, should be allowed in one class of Houses, and from £85 to £91 per annum should be allowed in another class of Houses, to commence from January 1874.

Secondly.—That the Special Commissioners, in answer to the recommendation of the Governing Body, stated that having gone fully into the case in the year 1872, they were scarcely prepared to re-open the question of charges for Board and Lodging.

Thirdly.—That the Chairman of the Governing Body informed you of the decision which was come to by the Special Commissioners.

Fourthly.—That on July 28th, the Governing Body received a communication from you, in which you stated that the Assistant Masters proposed to communicate with the Parents of the Boys under their care, and to inform them that it was no longer possible for them to continue the maintenance of their sons upon the present scale at the present rate, and that the reduction in the scale of maintenance necessary to be made would, as far as value was concerned, average nearly £4 a boy for each school time.

Fifthly.—That the Governing Body, on the receipt of your Letter, addressed an answer to you, in which they referred you to the Public Schools Act, Section 12, Sub-section 3, to the Regulations made in pursuance of that Act, and approved by the Special Commissioners, and to Statute XIX., Section 5, and stated it to be their opinion that any unauthorised increase in the face of these enactments would be illegal.

The Governing Body cannot but express their surprise and regret that, under the circumstances above stated, any such Circular as that which has been forwarded to the Parents of the Boys should have been issued, and, if possible, they still more regret that this should have been done with your knowledge and consent.

They deem it right to add that, as this Circular cannot now be formally withdrawn, it should be considered as issued without authority, and of no effect.

They, therefore, desire that you will have the goodness to inform the Assistant Masters of the unanimous conclusions which it has been the painful duty of the Governing Body to arrive at, and, for the future, they require that any application for an increased charge for the Board and Lodging of the Boys should be made in the first instance specifically to you, and, if approved by you, should be communicated to the Governing Body, without whose sanction it will be dereliction of duty for any one connected with the School to take independent action.

I am, Rev. Sir,

Your obedient Servant,

RICHARD COPE,

Clerk.

To the Head Master
    of Eton College.

The names of the body responsible for this document were :

The Provost of Eton, Rev. C. O. Goodford.

The Provost of King's, Rev. R. Okes.

The Very Rev. Robert Scott, Dean of Rochester.

Rev. W. H. Thompson, Master of Trinity College, Cambridge.

Sir G. G. Stokes, Bart., Lucasian Professor, Cambridge.

Rev. W. A. Carter.

Lord Lyttelton.

Earl of Morley.

John Hibbert.

Sir G. K. Rickards.

Though no record appears to exist of the circumstances which led to this outburst it may be conjectured that there was more behind it than meets the eye. The Provost and Fellows of the old College, now replaced by the new Governing Body, were practically all retired masters whose sympathies were likely to be on the side of their successors, and who had not exercised any very effective supervision over the fees charged by housemasters, dames and tutors. The fact that it was enacted in the new Governing Body's regulations that 'No Entrance Fee shall be paid by any boy for admission to a Boarding House'— a clause now omitted, presumably as being no longer necessary—suggests a certain lack of uniformity in the charges made in different houses. It was therefore probably essential that the Governing Body should establish the principle that no change should be made without their express consent in the payments made by parents. But the manner in which they did this was inexcusable, and those who remember Dr. Hornby will regret that his reply is not extant. At any rate, on December 4 of the same year he received a letter from the Provost, couched in a very different tone and allowing an additional charge to parents of half the sum suggested by the housemasters and making, besides, a small contribution out of the College Funds. Evidently the Governing Body had realised their mistake, but the episode serves to illustrate the troubles to which a Headmaster was liable. At the beginning of Dr. Warre's term of office similar troubles, but originating from another quarter, broke out again, as will be seen later. All Headmasters seem to be exposed to irresponsible criticism, and the more energetic the Headmaster is, the more he will be attacked. Dr. Lyttelton was a storm centre almost before he had left Haileybury, and Dr. Alington was hardly left in peace during the war, certainly never afterwards. But this is too recent history to be retailed here.

CHAPTER III

DR. WARRE CONFOUNDS HIS CRITICS

A genius for detail

The report issued in 1864 by the Public Schools Commissioners had suggested various matters that needed reform in the Eton system. It has been shown how far such reform had been carried by the first Headmaster appointed by the newly instituted Governing Body. All these innovations had been made while Dr. Warre [1] was a prominent assistant master, so that he had had ample time to consider the situation. In view of what he did for Eton it is interesting to recall the expectations aroused in different quarters by the news of his appointment. All who took any interest in Eton had up to this moment thought of him mainly in connection with Henley and the Volunteer movement. The boys in the school looked forward with glee to more facilities for rowing, cricket and sport in general, but expected that as far as work was concerned they would have a much easier time. A majority of the senior masters, in whose eyes the standard of classical scholarship among the boys outweighed all other considerations, held much the

---

[1] So named throughout ; he became a master in 1860, took Orders in 1867 and was made a D.D. in 1884.

same opinion and regarded his appointment with grave apprehension. The outside public, always suspicious of a new Headmaster, fell as usual into two camps ; one faction maintaining that nothing at Eton should ever be altered ; the other that because nothing ever was altered Eton was doomed. Among those who hold such conflicting views every Headmaster always has found and always must find a large number of violent and ill-informed critics who seem to spend their time in disseminating throughout London society the news that Eton is being ruined.

To this carping spirit full rein was given at the time of Dr. Hornby's resignation of the headmastership. On July 26, 1884, a few days before the date fixed for the meeting of the Provost and Fellows to select his successor, there appeared in *The Times* a letter, signed 'Academicus', from which the following extracts are taken. The second half of the letter contains a comparison between 'Mr. Warre' and 'Mr. Welldon', the two most prominent of the probable candidates, very much in favour of the latter. Of the former 'Academicus' writes :

'Mr. Warre is 47 years of age and has been for 24 years a master at Eton. In his youth he gained a Balliol scholarship, a First Class in the Final Schools, and a Fellowship at All Souls, but for the last quarter of a century he has made no mark as a scholar, a preacher, or a man of letters. His name is associated with no questions of educational reform ; on the other hand he is well known as the best rowing coach in England and as an able field-officer of Volunteers. He is an oppidan of the oppidans. The ordinary Etonian character, for good or for bad, has received a strong impression from his energy and strength of will.'

The sting of these remarks lies in what has been said in the earlier half of the letter. The writer is drawing a picture of Eton which was not and never had been true, though the exact converse of part of it might have been so fifty years earlier. Eton, he says,

'is made up of two schools, each with very different characteristics, the 70 collegers and the 800 oppidans. The smaller section has proved itself every year more moral, more industrious, more distinguished in academical honours ; the larger has become by degrees more idle, more extravagant, more self-indulgent, more entirely devoted to athletics and less to literary pursuits. It is scarcely a parody to say that an Eton collegian receives the best education in England, an Eton oppidan the worst. The choice of the new headmaster will determine which of these two principles is to triumph—whether the hard-working college spirit is to spread over the school this hardy nucleus, prove itself the Piedmont of Eton, or whether this little island of industry is to be swept away by the rising flood of pleasure-seeking and amusement.'

One of the main causes of the bitterness displayed is veiled in this letter, but revealed in another—also anonymous—which *The Times* published three days later. All this outburst of vituperation was the last, despairing cry of those who saw the old privileged position

55   E

of the Colleger who passed, as a matter of course, from Eton to King's and back from King's to Eton slipping away. One Oxford Oppidan they had endured—with sufficiently ill grace in some cases, as the letter below will show ; the idea of a second was more than they could stand. The style of this second writer is hardly equal to that of 'Academicus'.

'Before a "river coach",' he begins, 'is appointed to be headmaster of Eton, may I be allowed to mention one notorious fact ? No Colleger ever expected favour from Mr. Warre, unless he was Mr. Warre's pupil. At Eton the headmaster has no pupils. But he has more to do than any of his colleagues, except the master in college, with the 70 boys on the foundation. Half the division which he teaches in school necessarily consists of them. All of them are supposed to be under his peculiar care. I am not going to say anything in praise of the collegers, for I was one of them myself. They have been described on high authority as "intellectually the *élite* of the school." I have heard many an Eton master say that it was a pleasure and a privilege to teach them. They certainly form the working element of Eton. They come there with other objects than to amuse themselves. They cannot afford to be idle, extravagant, or ostentatious. They are necessarily, unless depressed and discouraged, an example of industry— a safeguard against Eton's becoming a mere intellectual infirmary. Mr. Warre never concealed his dislike for them, or his opinion that they were out of place in a great rowing and cricketing establishment. If the Governing Body agree with him there is no more to be said. They must, of course, know how much depends upon their decision to-morrow. If Eton does not adapt herself to modern requirements, there can be only one result. Her endowments are no more sacred than those of the City companies or the Established Church. Mr. Warre would not be a colourless neutral like Dr. Hornby, whom the most illustrious of Eton's sons [1] has set to preside over the greatest school in the world.'

The letters quoted are but a fraction of those which appeared during 1884 and 1885. It will be readily appreciated that the atmosphere created by such a correspondence in the public press rendered the position of the new Headmaster extremely difficult. Even after the appointment of Dr. Warre the attack was continued on a side issue. It had become necessary to improve the accommodation of the Collegers, and this necessitated the removal of the Hawtrey library. Various proposals were put forward, and the rumour got about that Upper School was to take its place, and that Savile House was to be pulled down to make way for a new speech-room. This called forth a torrent of expostulation and a letter to *The Times* signed by four hundred Old Etonians. A letter of seven lines from Dr. Hornby saying that the Governing Body had sanctioned none of these schemes except the improvement of the accommodation for Collegers did a good deal to put an end to this agitation, the only result of which was

---

[1] Presumably Mr. Gladstone, then Prime Minister.

to postpone the erection of an adequate library for twenty years. *Punch* had already summed up the situation with its usual acuteness in a letter accompanied by a drawing of a small Colleger standing in front of the entrance to School Yard :

> 'SIR,—In last week's number I saw your clever Artist's satirical, political, adaptation of Mr. Harding Cox's well known picture, *The Tug of War*, and it struck me, as it must have struck you, as an old Oppidan, that just now the true reading, from an Etonian point of view, would be "The 'Tug' of Warre", which will be intelligible to every one who has been brought up in the cool cloisters of "Henry's holy shade".'

Dr. Warre was not long in proving the absurdity of most of these anticipations. The boys were staggered by a spate of notices announcing the addition of new hours of work or the extension of old ones. Their view was well expressed by an ingenious drawing made by a boy then in Middle Division representing the old fable of King Log and King Stork with Dr. Hornby's head cut from a photograph and affixed to King Log and Dr. Warre's to King Stork. The masters were at any rate relieved of all anxiety as to their new Headmaster's determination to improve the work of the school. The only antagonism that survived came from a section of Sixth Form not clever enough to realise that Dr. Warre's scholarship, though completely different in character from Dr. Hornby's, was no less sound, and from the ultra-conservative faction of Old

Etonians. So virulent was the abuse of the latter, so galling the ostentatious boredom of the former, that at the end of a year Dr. Warre was near breaking-point, and late one night composed a letter of resignation. Luckily it was never sent, for next morning he determined not to give up the fight and the letter was torn up.

What were the reforms that aroused such sound and fury? One of the first was the abolition of the stupid system already mentioned under which the whole of Fifth Form Absence was called by the Headmaster. An immediate stop was put to this futile waste of time. The school was divided into five groups of roughly two hundred boys apiece, and the masters in desk were made responsible for the Absences of their respective groups. It is typical of the kind of criticism that greeted every change that even this salutary reform evoked an indignant letter to *The Eton College Chronicle*.

The next step had been long overdue. The growth in numbers of the school and the increasing complexity of its organisation required a more efficient form of administrative machinery than could be provided by the personal supervision of the Headmaster and the clerical efforts of his butler. A room, formerly used as a schoolroom, opening on to the colonnade under Upper School, was converted into an office. Sergeant-Major Osborne, of the E.C.R.V.,[1] was installed as school clerk and at once

---

[1] Eton College Rifle Volunteers. See Chapter XII, p. 220, and *Eton Book of the River*, p. 171.

showed his capacity for carrying out the detail of all the Headmaster's new arrangements.

How essential such an institution was is best shown by an outline of what it does to-day. For the sake of those who did not know Eton under Dr. Hornby it is necessary to add some explanation of the manner in which what is now the work of the office was performed—or in a good many cases left to chance.

Under Dr. Warre's predecessors each classical division had a Praepostor. The boys in the division held this office in rotation, usually for half a week. For each division there was a Praepostor book with spaces for the date and school and the division master's signature. Below these came subdivisions headed 'Out Afresh', 'Staying Out', 'Leave' and 'In Afresh'. All of these were on the left half of the page ; the right half, headed 'Excuses', was blank. After early school the Praepostor had to take his book to the house of each boy in the division who was 'Out Afresh', and get the reason of the boy's absence written in this blank space and duly signed by some responsible person. If it happened that these excuses had to be got for two or three boys in different houses in the interval between 8.30 and 9.15 (early school and chapel) the time for breakfast was reduced almost to vanishing point. In chapel the Praepostor had to mark all his division in, and, though in most cases each division sat together, the one placed on the altar steps had half a dozen boys whose seats were at the other end, and the luckless Praepostor had to speculate on their attendance. Failure to mark out any of the six entailed the writing of three hundred lines, as one of the authors of this book found to his cost. A boy, who at early school had stated that he would be in chapel, fell downstairs and hurt himself in the interval. The excuse that he could not see these boys was met with the cold rejoinder, 'Then you should have walked down and looked.' What would have been the fate of any small boy who had taken this literally, and advanced from the east end to meet the procession of Sixth Form marching into chapel from the west end, is best left to the reader's imagination.

The other author had an equally unfortunate experience in connection with Absence, when, as it came to the turn of his division to be called, the Praepostor had to go up and stand by the Head-master's side, hat, book and pencil in hand, ready to write down the names of fresh absentees, or to ejaculate 'Leave, sir,' or 'Staying out, sir,' when the name called was already in his book. The unlucky author had lost his Praepostor book—as had happened to many another—but had had the forethought to provide himself with a piece of paper to take its place. Nothing was said, and he thought all was well. But at the next Absence, two days later, as he was going away came the words, 'Are you the Praepostor who had no book last time ? Very careless of you ! Georgic !'

When mathematical schools were introduced and the classical divisions were redistributed into different and smaller groups, the Praepostors had to take their books round to each mathematical master who had

up to him any portion of their divisions, and Praepostor books are still extant in the Harcourt Collection
showing six or seven different signatures for a single
school.

Dr. Warre removed the most objectionable feature
of this system at once by transferring to the school
office the duty of collecting excuses for early school.
It was not till 1902 that Praepostors finally disappeared. During school hours messengers from
the school office collect from each division, whatever the subject, report forms, which take the
place of the old Praepostor book. In chapel boys
are marked in, pew by pew, by the occupant of the
end seat. For Absence the lists are prepared in the
office, with the names of those on leave or staying
out deleted. All this has only been rendered possible
by the fact that lists giving the names of all who are
sick or absent are collected from the houses between
7.30 and 8.30 every morning. Subsequent casualties
are reported by the dame as soon as possible, while
those boys who for any reason have leave off an
Absence have to bring a leave ticket duly signed
by the housemaster to the office before the Absence
list is prepared.

The name Praepostor still survives in the case of
the Headmaster's Praepostors. Members of Sixth
Form hold office in rotation, one Colleger and one
Oppidan each week. They summon boys wanted
for any purpose by the Headmaster, especially those
who have the misfortune to be 'in the bill'; those,
that is, who have committed any offence sufficiently

serious to be referred to him. A nice distinction exists between the two formulas by which the message is conveyed. Those whose crimes come in the less serious category are told that they are 'to go to the Headmaster after school'; but the words, 'Is So-and-so in this division? He's to stay,' are only used on the now rare occasions when So-and-so is to be beaten.

When the school office was first organised there was only one school messenger attached to it, an ex-rifleman named William Hall, known to many generations of boys as the Fusee. There are now several, and notes are collected and distributed from house to house three times a day, while each messenger is also in charge of a particular group of schoolrooms.

To give details of all the activities of the school office would be tedious, but a few instances will illustrate its extreme usefulness in a variety of ways. Till it came into existence a housemaster had no means of knowing whether an applicant for a vacancy in his house was entered on another list, and he might accidentally discover that a boy he was expecting had already gone to another house. If, on the other hand, he wanted to fill a chance vacancy, there was no means of discovering a boy who needed one. If at the beginning of a new Half a boy came back a few days late owing to illness, he could only find out to what masters he should go for various subjects by application to his tutor, and the tutor was unlikely to have kept the lists. Those who on leaving wished to have their names carved in Upper School had to unearth the Headmaster's butler and pay him a sovereign to get it done. Nowhere could any list be found to show what boys were in danger of superannuation, unless it were in a book kept by the Headmaster in which new boys inscribed their names, age and address during the progress of the entrance examination. School punishments had to be left in the Headmaster's pantry, those set by individual masters on some schoolroom or pupil-room desk, from which they were apt to disappear. Boys discovered as best they could in what schoolrooms they would find the masters in whose divisions they were placed each Half.

Nowadays the names of all boys entered for the school and the year of entry are recorded at the school office, and those concerned are immediately informed if the same boy is down for two houses. Another list is kept giving details of all boys who want a vacancy. The school clerk is an unfailing source of information as to divisions, schoolrooms and anything else a boy wants to know ; and, if he is not available, all the necessary lists are exhibited in a case outside the office. The same omniscient official is ready not only to arrange to have names carved on leaving, but to tell any applicant exactly where his family's names are carved and whether there is room for another to be added in the same place, for Captain Baker, while school clerk, compiled a list of all the names carved in any of the recognised positions, with the exception of Lower School.

Lists are also circulated to all masters showing what boys are already in danger of superannuation, and also what boys will be so, if they fail once in Trials. School punishments are shown up at the school office and duly marked off; and if the paper bears the name of an individual master, it is safely transmitted to him.

Nor is this all. Not so very many years ago masters who wanted to set proses, verses, unseens, grammar papers and so on to their divisions had either to get these printed or to dictate them. In the one case the cost, in the other the waste of time, were, cumulatively, considerable. Now the school office produces as many copies as may be required in less than twenty-four hours ; division lists and many examination papers are typed or reproduced by one of the various machines that exist for this kind of work, and in this way a good deal of expense is saved to the School Fund.

Another useful, though among boys unpopular, institution was only rendered possible by the creation of the school office. Those who are habitually unpunctual are condemned to sign their names, five minutes before early school begins, in a book kept there for the purpose. As this in many cases involves a considerable walk from the boy's house to the office and another from the office to his schoolroom, it serves as a very fair deterrent and at the same time avoids the imposition of 'lines' or some other equally unsatisfactory penalty. This book is known as the Tardy Book. In at least one case its existence suggested to a master (now retired) a refinement on the system, consisting in a demand for the delivery of a given number of plantains, extracted from his lawn, before early school. The present Headmaster has devised a further improvement. Old offenders who fail to sign their names are to be kept back twenty minutes on the Saturday of Long Leave or the first day of the holidays for each offence.

For many years boys whose names were on Tardy Book were unable to obtain any Leave. More recently the alteration in the whole system of Leave has rendered this additional penalty illogical, and the punctuality of both masters and boys is now so extraordinarily good compared to what it was even thirty years ago or less that it is unnecessary to treat delinquents so severely.

It has seemed advisable to dwell at some length on the subject of the school office, because those who have become masters since its institution are quite unable to understand how the school existed without it. On it depend innumerable odds and ends of organisation besides those mentioned. To enumerate them here would be impossible, but it is not too much to say that the universal practice of boys and masters alike may be summed up in the words, 'When in doubt apply to the school office'. For this Eton owes an immense debt of gratitude to the three men who have held the office of school clerk — Sergeant - Major Osborne, Sergeant - Major Gaffney and Captain A. C. Baker.

Another result of Dr. Warre's organising capacity was the introduction, or rather the re-introduction, of the Calendar. Something of the kind was published under the auspices of G. J. Dupuis, then a

Fellow, in 1842, and in the beginning of this first issue he wrote the following 'Notice' :

'The Lists of ETON SCHOOL were first printed and published in the year 1791, and have continued to appear, very nearly in their original form, annually, at each successive Election. Before that period Manuscript Lists were prepared once in each School-time by the Head Master, and presented by him to the Provost ; this custom still continues. In earlier times, "Bills" of the School, (as they were called,) written on long narrow rolls of paper or parchment, are the only memorials to be met with. They are of course extremely rare.

'It has been felt, that some useful improvements might be very well introduced, and added to the List of Names ; and it is in the hope of rendering some service in this respect, that the present "ETON CALENDAR" has been prepared.

'Should it meet with the approval of those who take an interest in Eton, and be found to be useful, it will be published at Election every year, with such additions and alterations as may from time to time be deemed expedient.

Eton College,   GEORGE JOHN DUPUIS.
   July 23rd, 1842.'

The ten copies of this Calendar known to exist cover the years from 1842 to 1852. Each contains a statement that the College was founded in 1441 and that the 'Society', as it is called, consisted of the 'Provost, seven Fellows, two Masters, two Conducts, seventy Scholars, an Organist, ten Lay Clerks, ten Choristers, a Clerk, a Sexton, a Steward of the Courts, a Registrar, fourteen Servants and ten

Almswomen'. The qualifications required for the position of Provost, Fellow or Scholar are also given, including one to the effect that Scholars must be born in England, to the exclusion of Scotland and Ireland. Other items are lists of the Provosts from the foundation of the school, and of Head and Lower Masters from 1660 ; a table of the comparative numbers of the school at different dates ; and details of the various scholarships available and the terms of the bequests under which they were held. Incidentally, these details reveal the fact that the Merton Postmasterships, printed in the list of Honours at the Universities in the modern Calendar as the Chambers Postmasterships, were founded by John Chamber, Esq., and that the *s* is therefore intrusive.

In the first of these old Calendars there is a frontispiece showing a rather attractive view of Chapel. In all of them there are Almanacks for the ensuing school year. In these there are one or two curious features. At the beginning of each schooltime three dates are given, that of the opening of the school, that of the return of the Collegers and Lower Oppidans, and, lastly, that of the Sixth Form Oppidans. These are separated by five or six days from one another. For instance, in 1851 the dates for the winter schooltime are September 1, 6, and 13. On December 10 the school closed. These peculiarities may be a survival from the days when transport was uncertain, or may be based on the University distinction between Term and Full Term. Another point worth noting is that Saturday is the only day in the week printed as a 'Half Holyday'. Presumably on Tuesdays and Thursdays there was 'Play at Four', *i.e.* no school after 3 o'clock chapel. This clashes with the accepted idea that Tuesday was a whole holiday, Thursday a half-holiday, with 'Play at Four' on Saturday. But the problem is outside the period covered by this book.

Two or three of these Calendars came out while Dr. Warre was still a boy at Eton, so it is not surprising that as soon as he became Headmaster in 1884 he set to work to produce a book on the same lines. How thoroughly his work was done is shown by a comparison of his first Calendar (1885) with those now in existence. Alterations and additions have been made to suit the changes in the school, but, *mutatis mutandis*, nine-tenths of what he inserted still remain.

Allusion has been made to an alteration in the system of leave. In Dr. Hornby's time boys were allowed one Long Leave and two Short Leaves each Half. Long Leave ordinarily began after the third school on the Saturday, and boys had to be back in time for the corresponding school on the Monday. If the Saturday happened to be a holiday, they could go away after early school ; similarly, if a holiday fell on the Monday they were not required to be back till lock-up. Boys and their parents selected any week-end that suited them. Short Leave began after early school on a whole holiday, after twelve on a half-holiday, and ended at 10 P.M. This system continued up to Dr. Warre's retirement, except that he cut off one Short Leave. Dr. Lyttelton a year after his appointment began to limit the choice of dates for Long Leave. After some experiments he introduced the present system whereby in the two winter schooltimes a holiday is transferred to a Monday in the middle of the Half and no other date is permissible for Long Leave. In the summer Long Leave is confined to the week-end of the match at Lord's, and ends on the Monday evening.

Of Dr. Warre's reforms the most important after the creation of the school office are, firstly, the institution of Trials [1] for all boys every Half and, secondly, the substitution of German for Greek in the upper part of the school for those boys who showed no aptitude for the classics or to whom modern languages were for some reason particularly needful.

Up to 1884 boys had only had to pass an examination test once a year. In the other two Halves masters set their own divisions a few papers on the work they had been doing. The result of this examination—which went by the name of Collections—did not in any way affect promotion or offer any incentive to work. Dr. Warre's system, which has remained substantially unchanged ever since, ensures that the duller or idler boys know that at the end of every schooltime they have got to clear another fence, and gives to the cleverer and harder working an opportunity of showing their capacity and earning some distinction.

The replacement of Greek by German, though not in itself a very revolutionary measure, was the first

[1] For further details as to the organisation of Trials, see pp. 162 ff. and 261 ff.

step in a change of system which has gradually been carried further and further, till now in the two top blocks of the school, containing 321 boys, history provides the main subject of study for 118, modern languages for 62, Latin and Greek for 48, mathematics and science for 38 ; the remaining 55 are working for either the school certificate or some other examination. The gradual evolution of the present curriculum, together with some details of its scope, will be found in Chapter V.

Dr. Warre's reforms, in so far as they dealt with the educational and administrative organisation of the school, were completed during the first five years of his headmastership, though he never relaxed his efforts to improve the standard of efficiency of masters and boys alike. From 1890 up to the date of his retirement the framework which he had devised remained unaltered. In the early years of the present century he came to the conclusion that it was time to advance another step, and he was contemplating further changes as revolutionary as those with which he had begun. In the summer of 1904 he acquainted the Provost and Fellows with his intention. They considered that at his age he would be better advised to leave any drastic alterations to a successor. Dr. Warre was deeply moved by this intimation of their opinion. He wrote a letter resigning his position, and announced in Chambers at the beginning of the next Half that he had done so. 'If I am standing in the way of the good of the school', he said, 'it is time for me to go.'

It was perhaps unfortunate that he was not allowed to complete his work. No one who had not had his unbroken experience of the working of the system established twenty years before could possibly understand so well the needs of the situation and the methods by which they could be met. Dr. Warre, moreover, had a breadth of vision and a grasp of detail rarely found together. His capacity for work was prodigious. Day after day, if not in school, he could be found at almost any hour in his study, ready to turn from the work on which he was engaged to whatever question might be brought before him by some member of the staff. As an assistant master with a large boys' house and a full pupil-room—and what the latter meant is described in Chapter VIII— he commanded the Corps, looked after the river, managed all the 'passings' and coached the Eight, and this at a time when there were no motor-cars or bicycles to take him rapidly from point to point. Only those who have tried to cope with any one of these tasks can fully realise what the combination of all of them in one man's hands entailed. This untiring energy he transferred on becoming Headmaster to the duties of that office, and by his example inspired at any rate the younger members of his staff with the desire to live up to the standard which he set. To his work Eton owes the position that enabled his successors to carry the school safely through the troublous times that began ten years after his resignation.

CHAPTER IV

DR. LYTTELTON AND DR. ALINGTON

Experiments and patchwork

At the moment of Dr. Warre's retirement the trend of educational development throughout the country was beginning, as has been shown, to suggest that further changes were required. Dr. Warre had realised the position and had already partly decided how to deal with it. But no successor, however capable, could possibly, for some years after his appointment, pick up all the threads of the situation and settle what alterations were needed. The new Headmaster, whoever he might be, would have to familiarise himself with the complicated details of organisation in all the subjects taught in each part of the school; to devote much time, as was then thought necessary, to the teaching of Sixth Form; to make the acquaintance of a staff of sixty masters; form an opinion of their respective capacities and the soundness, or unsoundness, of their judgment; get into touch with the leading boys in the school and win their confidence and respect; and deal with the thousand and one petty affairs that the conduct of a great school brings before him every day. What these mean Dr. Alington has described with his usual vivacity in *Things Ancient and Modern* (p. 209).

73

Until all such matters had become a matter of mere routine, a new Headmaster would have neither the knowledge nor the time required for working out a new scheme. With the arrival, therefore, of Dr. Lyttelton the school inevitably entered upon a period of experiment. Something had to be done, but the Headmaster was not in a position to discriminate readily between the numerous suggestions with which he was assailed from all sides.

The change made at this time in the arrangements for Long Leave has already been mentioned (see Chapter III, p. 70). But the real problem with which Dr. Lyttelton was faced was, what was to be the position of subjects other than the classics in the education of boys in general. It has been shown how in the previous half-century mathematics, modern languages and science had forced their way into the curriculum. Of these, however, mathematics alone was allowed a satisfactory proportion of the school hours in every block ; and even in this subject no adequate provision was made for specialists. The ever-increasing demand for more modern education had been to some extent met in two ways. During four hours in the week—called Extra Studies—boys in First Hundred were offered a wide range of subjects from which they could make their choice of any two. Besides this, boys in Fifth Form could for a small additional fee take Extras, that is, get private instruction out of school in anything that members of the staff could teach. Though these arrangements to some extent acted as a palliative, they involved serious disadvantages. Boys were encouraged to look on time spent with a master as the chief criterion of serious work ; extra fees are always unsatisfactory ; and, worst of all, too many subjects might be studied simultaneously ; for the boy who was learning German and science in Extra Studies and French in Extras still had to do in school a large amount of Latin and Greek if he was going to the University, to say nothing of mathematics, divinity and history.

Having assumed office, Dr. Lyttelton almost immediately made two changes of the utmost importance. In 1906 it was announced that Greek would no longer be required of boys entering the school. This, though it aroused much criticism at the time, was the first and most obvious step towards the reduction of the number of subjects that boys of all standards of capacity were expected to learn, and anticipated by thirteen years the action of the authorities of Oxford and Cambridge[1] in abolishing Greek as a compulsory subject in Responsions and the Previous Examination. Secondly, he co-ordinated the work of the two top blocks in the school so far as to render it possible for boys who had obtained a school certificate to abandon classical work and specialise in mathematics, modern languages, science or history. The result was that at the beginning of the third year of his headmastership there were about fifty boys at the top of the school doing no classical work at all, while in Army Class, the numbers

[1] Cambridge 1919, Oxford 1920.

of which had been steadily growing, there were rather over a hundred more whose education in this direction was confined to five or six hours a week of Latin.

That the ideas underlying these changes were sound can hardly be denied ; the early stages of education were freed from the shackles of a narrow convention, and the later stages catered for every kind of intellectual bent. That the results have been less satisfactory than might have been anticipated is, unfortunately, almost equally certain. Relieved of the burden of Greek, boys coming on from their preparatory school should have been better grounded than before in Latin, French, mathematics and history. But no one whose experience dates back to the nineteenth century can doubt that, far from improving, the average standard of attainment among boys of twelve and thirteen is worse all round than it was. Reduction in the number of subjects demanded in the later stages might have compensated for this lack of knowledge at the start ; but the regulations of the Public Schools Commission have only replaced one bogey by another—Greek by science ; and the efficiency of modern science masters exacts a standard of work in this subject unknown to the generation to which a science school was an opportunity for somnolent relaxation or rowdy in-discipline. So the improvement in the position has been more superficial than real.

At this point it may be well to restate the problem that awaited and still awaits solution. Under the old system nearly all boys acquired a very fair knowledge of two subjects—Greek and Latin. The standard attained was satisfactory, but to a large proportion of those taught the subjects were uninspiring. Nowadays the choice of subjects is wide enough to rouse the interest of anyone who wishes to learn anything ; but their number is so great that only the more highly gifted ever get beyond the initial drudgery inseparable from any study. Dr. Lyttelton provided a foundation on which a solid edifice might be reared. But owing to war and other difficulties nothing has been added to it but a temporary patchwork.

Just about the time when he became Headmaster the authors of this book propounded a scheme which did at least attempt to avoid the two main pitfalls of education—multiplicity of subjects and failure to attract more than one type of capacity. It is perhaps worth while to explain briefly the methods by which they endeavoured to find a compromise between the old system and the new, free from the shortcomings which make both to some extent un-satisfactory. For this purpose the curriculum was divided into three groups. In one group Latin and Greek were the main subjects, in a second French and German, in a third mathematics and science. In each group two-thirds of the hours in school— that is, under the Eton system, about sixteen hours— were allotted to these main subjects. The remaining one-third—eight hours—provided for two minor subjects intended to give a properly balanced education, so that those whose main study was linguistic and literary should have a fair proportion of mathematics and science, and *vice versa*. The following conspectus may serve to make the framework of the scheme clearer. The main subjects in each branch included the necessary minimum of divinity and history.[1]

CLASSICAL BRANCH

Main Subjects (16 hrs.) $\left\{\begin{array}{l}\text{Latin} \\ \text{Greek}\end{array}\right.$

Minor Subjects (8 hrs.) $\left\{\begin{array}{l}a. \\ b.\end{array}\right\}$ *e.g.* Mathematics, Science or French

MODERN LANGUAGE BRANCH

Main Subjects (16 hrs.) $\left\{\begin{array}{l}\text{French} \\ \text{German}\end{array}\right.$

Minor Subjects (8 hrs.) $\left\{\begin{array}{l}a. \\ b.\end{array}\right\}$ *e.g.* Mathematics, Science or Latin

MATHEMATICAL-SCIENTIFIC BRANCH

Main Subjects (16 hrs.) $\left\{\begin{array}{l}\text{Mathematics} \\ \text{Science}\end{array}\right.$

Minor Subjects (8 hrs.) $\left\{\begin{array}{l}a. \\ b.\end{array}\right\}$ *e.g.* Latin, French or German

At what point in a school career the divergence to these different branches should take place depends on a variety of considerations. Of these the chief is the objective of the bulk of the boys passing through the school. At Eton, for instance, roughly 60 per cent.

[1] See Chapter V, pp. 96, 97.

proceed to Oxford or Cambridge. As long as these Universities make Latin or Greek obligatory, a considerable amount of time must be spent on one or other of these subjects until the School Certificate is passed. For those going to Oxford a second language is also a necessity. To relegate languages to an inferior position with only four hours a week each is therefore practically impossible except in the case of the cleverer boys. To those who agree with the authors that the basis of education should be linguistic or literary the conclusion is obvious. It is unwise to devote two-thirds of the school hours to mathematics and science till a boy is at least fifteen years of age. As long, then, as conditions remain unchanged, it seems inevitable that the introduction of the mathematics and science branch should be postponed till after the school certificate has been taken. For those who wish to offer science as one of their subjects in this examination it would have to be substituted for one of their languages.

Consideration of this scheme and of various modifications of it continued for four or five years. A time-table was worked out which showed that it was practicable without interfering with the composition of the existing staff, and that when the transition stage was over it would be economical in teaching power. The scheme was eventually abandoned with some reluctance by its authors owing to Dr. Lyttelton's fear that unless Latin was retained as the basis of the curriculum the entry of dull boys into the Universities would be endangered.

This negative result was not reached till the end of 1911. A few minor changes in the allotment of hours to different subjects were then made, but after 1906 in spite of many discussions and experiments no radical reform was introduced. In 1914 war put an end to all development and in 1916 Dr. Lyttelton resigned. It may be worth noting that he was the last Headmaster who confined to the top classical division the teaching in school which was still regarded as one of his main duties.

The last two or three years of Dr. Lyttelton's headmastership were, as just said, overshadowed by the war ; and for the same reason it may be doubted whether any Headmaster in the history of the school ever assumed office under more difficult conditions than Dr. Alington, who succeeded to the position in January 1917. The school had shrunk in the preceding year to 985 boys, in which number were included thirty or forty Belgian refugees who for the purposes of work were mostly organised apart from the rest of the school under the control of a Belgian barrister, M. Renier. Owing to this drop in numbers and steadily rising prices the financial position was extremely difficult ; but this for the moment affected housemasters more than the school as a whole. The feeding of the boys also presented many problems to all concerned. Military training demanded an unusual amount of time and organisation. Last, but not least, the staff was depleted by the absence of about twenty masters who were serving at the front, of whom four had been killed. No able-bodied young men were available to fill their places, and, especially at a time when all boys knew that their chance of reaching the age of twenty was small and were anxious to get as much as possible out of life while it lasted, the inclusion of so many temporary masters, who for one reason or another frequently left after a brief period of service, was bound to have a bad effect on instruction and discipline alike. Nor did these difficulties vanish with the end of the war. Of the young men of three or four and twenty, who would in ordinary circumstances have been ready to become masters, those not killed or disabled had been employed since leaving school in military positions ; most of them needed a rest to enable them to recuperate after the strain they had undergone ; and besides this they had to spend two or three years in completing their scholastic education. Dr. Alington had therefore been Headmaster for at least five years before he could begin to bring his staff up to anything like its usual standard. In these circumstances he could not have made any drastic changes in the curriculum, even if he had wished. The one important alteration that he introduced was to enable boys for whom a completely classical education was undesirable to drop Latin and keep up Greek, whereas in his predecessor's time such boys had been tied to Latin. Apart from this he confined his attention to the improvement of the arrangements for specialists with such success that in a few years their number was doubled.

As regards finance, on the other hand, he

revolutionised the whole system. Up to 1921 the parents of those who required extra tuition in any special subject or incurred any exceptional expense owing to illness had to bear the cost in addition to the ordinary school fees. About this time Dr. Alington found himself faced with a new situation. The cost of living and of the provision of new buildings or the upkeep of old ones had increased enormously. But owing to the same state of affairs and to the high rate of taxation many parents were finding it difficult to keep their sons at Eton. Simultaneously the College, which had in the past paid a good deal more than its share of the school expenses, found that its income was for the future likely to be exceeded by its expenditure by a sum amounting to not much less than £10,000 a year. This change in its financial position was due to a variety of causes. In the previous half-century College had acquired the freehold of all house property at Eton and had built a considerable number of new houses and schoolrooms, besides improving and adding to existing ones. To raise the rents of these to an economic figure would have been to hit still harder masters who were already suffering severely from the financial conditions caused by the war. Under the terms of the leases College had made itself responsible for all structural repairs, and since 1900 it had treated its tenants generously in other respects. Consequently, far from being an asset as before the war, these houses had become a liability. Secondly, owing to the increase of the staff and the institution of compulsory retirement for most masters at the age of fifty-five, pensions had become a very serious item in the accounts. Rates on College buildings had increased largely. On the other hand the income derived from landed property had seriously diminished.

During and for a year or two after the war the adverse consequences of such a situation had not made themselves apparent, as expenditure had been of necessity curtailed to a minimum owing to the impossibility of getting materials or labour. But the accumulation of arrears and the result of their postponement only aggravated the situation when the time came for dealing with them.

At this juncture Dr. Alington proposed that the whole system of payments should be altered, and that an inclusive fee should be charged, covering practically all the items that had previously appeared under the heading of compulsory or voluntary extras, and also providing for a large amount of the expenditure involved in cases of illness. Unfortunately, when he persuaded the Provost and Fellows to accept this scheme, the latter had not fully realised the seriousness of the position, thinking, probably, in common with most people at the time, that these conditions were but temporary and that in another year or two the College would again be solvent. Consequently the new fee was fixed too low, but in spite of this the scheme was so sound financially that equilibrium was almost restored and for twelve years the College and the School Fund jointly were enabled to meet ordinary current expenditure with a small balance on the right side. How invaluable the time thus gained has proved was only fully demonstrated in the monetary stress of 1931 and the following years. The fees were raised in 1936, though even then this would not have been necessary but for the demand by a considerable and influential body of Old Etonian parents for a higher standard of accommodation in boys' houses, which has necessarily involved a large expenditure on bricks and mortar.

The same principle that led to Dr. Alington's establishment of an inclusive fee was soon afterwards applied to the various small sums which had formerly been collected from boys in cash for various athletic pursuits. All these were lumped together in a sum of £4, subsequently raised to £5, annually.

It is almost impossible to convey to anyone who has not worked under him and with him the value to Eton of Dr. Alington's seventeen years as Headmaster. Most of the famous Headmasters at Eton or elsewhere have gained their reputation by concentrating their efforts at reform on some particular and often limited objective. Dr. Alington's versatility was such that there was no direction in which he did not make his influence felt, and that there is now hardly any subject or institution that does not owe something to his active and stimulating interest.

Of the great alteration for the better that took place in his time in the external aspect of several parts of Eton more will be said in another chapter ; but over one side of school life his influence was unique. Only those who remember the general indifference of boys forty or fifty years ago to Chapel services and sermons and everything connected with them can appreciate the extent of the change. The whole attitude of the present generation to such matters seems to have been transformed. The most striking testimony to this is provided by the crowd seen in chapel at an early communion service on Sundays and the two or three special saints' days when there is no early school. In winter and summer alike, though the boys have the alternative of a rarely possible long lie, an enormous majority of those who have been confirmed get up and go to chapel entirely voluntarily. The development has been to some extent gradual. There is in boys a great fund of religious feeling, but it is usually hidden beneath an outer crust of shyness. Dr. Alington's methods of presenting the facts of religion to his congregation succeeded in breaking through this crust and caused boys no longer to be ashamed of what they really had always felt. How far this external change has affected the general life of the school no one except those who are boys at the moment can say for certain ; and they have no standard of comparison with earlier times. To those who have known the school formerly as boys and who know it now as masters it certainly appears that the modern generation is more considerate, more open-minded, more thoughtful.

That the form of the services and of the boys' view

of them have altered is undeniable. The services are briefer, brighter and more congregational.[1] The boys are more attentive and take an infinitely larger part in them. That some of the credit for this improvement is due to others, notably to Dr. Ley, the Precentor, and his predecessors from Dr. Barnby onwards, Dr. Alington would be the first to admit. But his example and his influence have furnished the motive power, while his own preaching has been very largely responsible for the final result. Among the Headmasters of the past sixty years it is doubtful whether even Dr. Warre did more for the good of the school.

In 1933 Dr. Alington accepted the Deanery of Durham and was succeeded by Mr. C. A. Elliott. Of the headmastership of the latter it is of course too early to speak, but three points may be noted. He is the first Headmaster not in Holy Orders and the first for nearly two hundred years chosen from outside the ranks of schoolmasters. He is also the first Headmaster who has recognised that under modern conditions of ever-increasing complexity the organisation and administration of a school of over eleven hundred boys requires all the time at any one man's disposal, and that to spend most of the morning and a good part of the night in teaching Sixth Form and correcting their exercises is incompatible with effective supervision of finance and attention to his other duties.

[1] The present Provost, the Rt. Hon. Lord Hugh Cecil, is trying to carry this movement still further.

86

CHAPTER V

SUBJECTS TAUGHT

An overloaded curriculum

The history of the gradual widening of a system of education which had included practically nothing but Latin and Greek has already been traced. For the sake of clearness it is perhaps well to repeat that it was not till 1869 that mathematics, French and science appeared in the regular curriculum of the school, and that even then mathematics had only three, French two and science one or two schools a week allotted to them. Nor did their position in this respect improve till in 1885 Dr. Warre gave a fourth school to mathematics, while in 1906 Dr. Lyttelton further recognised the claims of French by doubling the number of schools assigned to it. Until the school certificate has been obtained, the number of hours given to these two subjects has, with slight variations, remained unchanged up to the present time.

Meanwhile science had fallen from its already low estate and was only taught to a few specialists at the top of the school, till in 1907 it was discovered that this state of affairs contravened the regulations of the Public Schools Commissioners, who fifty years previously had ordained 'that every Boy shall learn Natural Science continuously from his entrance into

the Remove until he become one of the senior Boys
in the school, unless his Parent or Guardian express
in writing a desire for exemption from this Regulation'. At what stage a Boy becomes a senior Boy
must be left, as it was by the Commissioners, to the
reader's imagination.

To rectify this breach of the law Dr. Lyttelton in
1906 added science to the subjects taught in Remove
and Fourth Form, while a year or two later two hours
were also given to this subject in Lower Division.
In 1910 it was abolished in Fourth Form, and an
additional hour was given to Lower Division, while
ten years later a fourth hour was added in this block.

From this latter date (1920) the teaching of
science began to make rapid strides. At first the
increase in the number of boys taking it was most
marked at the top of the school. In 1914, including
boys in Army Class, there were about 60 making this
one of their main subjects. In 1920 there were about
140. The science staff gradually grew from five in
1914 to nine or ten from 1922 onwards. Nor was
science confined to physics and chemistry. Biology
had long been a possible alternative, though singularly few boys availed themselves of the opportunity.
A movement was now set on foot for giving some
training in agriculture. Mr. James Luddington
generously provided the money for the endowment
of two 'Land Prizes', and a master was appointed to
teach such boys as wished to study scientific methods
of farming. But the agricultural depression which
began two or three years after the war rather damped

enthusiasm for this subject, so that up to the present time not more than half a dozen boys in any given year have taken advantage of the facilities offered in this direction. So the bulk of the scientific training still consists of physics and chemistry ; and the present position is that there are 35 science special- ists in the two top blocks of the school doing from eleven to fifteen hours science a week ; 43 boys in Middle Division intending to take science in the school certificate and doing five hours a week ; while the whole of Lower Division, consisting of 243 boys, do four hours. Besides this all boys in Remove, 221 in all, do two hours. The figures are taken from the Calendar for the Michaelmas Half, 1935.

The demands of science, then, have been not illiberally met, though those concerned with the teaching of this subject will probably not subscribe to this view. Science is, perhaps inevitably, the most expensive form of education in the public school curriculum. Very large sums have been spent on laboratories, and the demand for new and increas- ingly costly plant seems unending, putting a great strain on financial resources. From the nature of the subject it is probably impossible to teach large classes. At Eton, at any rate in the three top blocks, the divisions taken in this subject are on the average slightly smaller than in mathematics and considerably smaller than in other subjects ; so that no compensa- tion for the cost of the plant required can be found in this direction.

That the results of the attempt to carry out the

ruling of the Commissioners of 1864 by teaching science to practically all boys in the school are in any way commensurate with the time, money and trouble expended is very hard to believe. Dr. Alington in *Things Ancient and Modern* has summed up the position most forcibly as regards both science and mathematics.

'The literary boy', he writes, 'should be required to know some arithmetic, and possibly some geometry : to demand algebra from him is to provoke dangerous reprisals.

'When we come to Science I am very anxious that he should be given some knowledge, but very certain that he should be given it in a different way from that which is rightly ordained for his scientific brother. Thousands of boys are at present doing experiments in expensive laboratories who know beforehand what to expect in view of the known nature of the materials they are handling and the known quantity of their own incompetence. I doubt whether this is education.'

Dr. Alington adds that the last two sentences are quoted from a speech made by him before the Royal Institution, and that they had then met with general agreement.

For a vigorous and convincing statement of his views on the whole question the reader must be referred to the volume from which the passage just quoted is taken. But his conclusion is much the same as has been more than once stated above : namely, that it is folly, almost criminal folly, to try to teach more than a very general outline of scientific discoveries and an elementary modicum of mathematics to boys who have no scientific or mathematical bent.

Nor is it less idiotic to force nothing but literary and linguistic studies on boys of mathematical and scientific proclivities ; but this statement needs some qualification ; for mathematics and science, unaided, cannot provide a liberal education.

In the first place every boy, no matter what his bent or intended career, is better educated—better fitted, that is, for whatever position he is to hold after leaving school—if, either on paper or aloud, he can express himself clearly and effectively in his own language. For boys of average intelligence it is doubtful whether any training is better calculated to achieve this object than that given by the translation of a foreign language into idiomatic English, and of idiomatic English into a foreign language. Whether the language chosen be ancient or modern is for this purpose of little consequence. A dead language has the advantages of simplicity and stability. It is not constantly acquiring new words and idioms. On the other hand, its apparent lack of any obvious usefulness is apt to render it unpalatable to boys of a practical turn of mind, and it offers a better target to the cheap criticism of those who have left school quite unconscious of what they owe to a classical training. Modern languages are free from the charge of uselessness, and many of them offer, in their early stages, fewer difficulties to the learner. Moreover a language that appeals to the ear and the imitative faculties may arouse in boys who have seemed unable to acquire knowledge by the usual methods of paper, pen and print an intelligence that would otherwise have remained undeveloped. But the grammatical rules of twenty or thirty years ago have in some cases been altered by modern usage and a number of words now current are not to be found in early dictionaries ; and this may occasionally lead to confusion.

As a means of education, then, there is not much to choose between the dead and the living languages. But, because they have no practical utility, public opinion is to a large extent prejudiced against the former and the idler is thus provided with a specious excuse for his idleness ; it is therefore perhaps better to cut the ground from under the feet of this section, at least, of the less intelligent majority and to let them show how hard they are prepared to work at something that they must admit to be useful. If taught on right lines French and German can provide a very satisfactory alternative to Latin and Greek. It cannot, however, be too much emphasised that, as an educational medium properly so called, they lose all their value if teachers yield to the temptation to take short cuts to a superficial familiarity such as enables the pupil to conduct an intelligible conversation in them on topics that only require a vocabulary of two or three hundred common words learnt parrot-like without any substantial knowledge of the grammar, structure or literature of the language. The jockey or commercial traveller who has spent two or three months in France or Germany can acquire this facility, though he may not be, in any real sense of the word, educated.

Of the subjects generally grouped under the heading of English subjects—essay-writing, précis, English literature, history and geography—something has already been said. It remains to examine them in more detail.

The writer of an essay should know most of what there is to know of his subject and should be able to approach it from some new point of view, to throw new light on the facts with which it deals, or to draw from them some new conclusions. Such qualifications are obviously bound to be lacking in the average schoolboy. The result is that he must either try to spin out the two or three things that he knows about his subject to a length quite disproportionate to their importance, or he must be supplied with a summary of the subject by his teacher, in which case his essay becomes a rather dull exercise in expansion. The subjects of which he may know something—cricket, football and the like—are soon exhausted, and are in any case not of a nature to inspire the essay writer. Regarded as a mere means towards teaching boys to express platitudes in correct English there may be something to be said for such essays. As literary productions or as examination tests they are a lamentable failure. Correct English can be far better learnt in other ways ; it has already been shown that a foreign language properly taught gives ample scope for this. Without more knowledge and more experience of life than falls to the lot of the average able-bodied boy of under eighteen or nineteen years of age essay-writing is a waste of time. Admittedly an exception must be made to this rather sweeping general statement in favour of the historical essay. But for this a boy is either allowed to get his information out of books, or has it previously supplied to him in some form of lecture. In the hands of an able boy a discussion of the facts he has been told in earlier lessons is admirable both as a test of memory and an exercise in English. But even these in the case of the less intelligent who are the subject of this chapter are apt to become rather tame summaries of what the master has said.

Précis-writing is not open to these objections, and, if the right sort of documents are chosen, may be made a very useful means of training boys to select the right points and to arrange them in the right order. The old précis of correspondence set in the Army examination or the rather thrilling story that has taken its place in more recent times are both admirably selected. Unluckily those responsible for the school certificate examinations have acquired the habit of putting before their unfortunate victims passages of unutterable dreariness written on topics outside the purview of the ordinary boy and couched in language much of which is barely intelligible to him. On the whole, as a means of education, a series of letters dealing with some episode in history, unfamiliar, but of a date not too remote, such as the Fashoda incident or the extradition of Jabez Balfour, is the best way of teaching a boy to discard what is of slight importance and to set out in simple English and clear chronological order the salient facts mentioned in the correspondence. The addition of an index gives an admirable training in neatness and orderliness, and helps materially to teach a boy first to comprehend and then to express in ten or twelve words the theme of each letter : in other words, to grasp the meaning of what he reads and to summarise it briefly and lucidly.

The teaching of literature as a regular lesson is a difficult and in some ways a dangerous undertaking. It is much easier to inspire dislike than appreciation of an author in the minds of those who are inclined to regard any work as distasteful. Probably the most successful process is occasionally, as a change from the usual routine, to read aloud some dramatic or comical passage of a kind likely to appeal to immature minds, sometimes to let boys choose their own passage and declaim it to the division, leaving the judging and apportionment of marks to those of the division who form the audience. The success of such a system, however, depends on the good will of the boys and their readiness to fall in with the spirit of the game. A nice, ugly, snub-nosed boy with a mop of red hair and noticeably large, ungainly feet, fairly brought the house down, in the recollection of one of the authors, when he led off with Calverley's lines : 'They tell me I am beautiful, they praise my silken hair, My little feet that silently slip on from stair to stair !' Another of the same division, who had already made his mark when he was killed in action at Boesinghe at the age of 24, roused many who heard him to read more of Rudyard Kipling's poetry by his rendering of 'The Grave of the Hundred Head'. On quite a different occasion another who has risen to a high position caused Homeric laughter by leading off with the first line of the same poem in a new guise—'There's a sleepy widow in Chester' : a slip that might provide a text for a lecture on the importance of the choice of epithets and the order of words. But such methods of instruction depend on the co-operation of the boys, and three or four by trying to introduce a spirit of disorder can render abortive the attempt to show that even the comparative dullard can find real pleasure in good prose and poetry.

In history a great revolution has taken place during the period under review. The old generation concentrated on the history of our own country, especially on its dates, its dynasties, its wars and its leading statesmen. This system tended to foster a complete lack of appreciation of the relative importance at any given date of England and other countries. It has been abandoned in the last quarter of a century and replaced by an attempt, firstly, to give an outline of the early history of other countries and to show the influence on it of climate and natural conditions ; and secondly, to trace the social development of our own country, principally in its relation to the rest of Europe and the colonial empire.

This is a topic of such magnitude as to be

beyond the range of knowledge of any but an expert of the first class, and still more beyond the scope of the ordinary pupil. In the hands of a born teacher with the necessary training it is capable of stirring almost enthusiastic interest among the young in the bearing of the world's past history on its present condition and in the probable evolution of its social progress. It also provides ample opportunity for lessons in the statement of views and the proper marshalling of facts ; it gives an excellent training in the observation of the influence of events in one country on the history of another ; and inculcates a due sense of proportion as regards the importance of different nations. Its defects are a tendency to engender the habit of theorising on insufficient data, and of considering that ingenious special pleading may take the place of accurate reasoning, especially where lack of certainty about many events makes it difficult to say that one view is superior to another. It was on these grounds that a very wise man who was himself an eminent historian deprecated to one of the authors the movement, then in its infancy, for the inclusion of more history in the ordinary school curriculum. 'Boys,' he said, 'while at school, should be taught subjects in which there is a clear-cut line between the right and wrong answer. History is a series of guesses at the most probable.'

To add geography as a separate subject to the already overladen school curriculum is a mistake. It falls into two natural divisions—historical and scientific. The former should be dealt with as an integral part of the teaching of history, and, as has been said above, the teachers of history of the modern school are endeavouring to give it its proper place. Some instruction in the scientific side of it should certainly be given to boys who are not going to make science their main subject. What the other components of such a course should be it is for scientists to settle. But it surely would not be hard for an expert to devise a programme that would reveal to boys in an interesting form the practical results that have ensued from the discovery of radium, of anæsthetics and various serums, of rays visible and invisible; the increase of knowledge concerning the composition of the earth and its relation to the rest of the universe; the function of birds and insects in the fertilisation of plants; and the harnessing of electrical forces. Such a list could be prolonged almost indefinitely; but the point to be borne in mind is that it is not proposed that a non-scientific boy should have a detailed knowledge of all or any of these matters, but that his powers of observation should be stimulated so that he may recognise his own ignorance and may have at any rate some idea of how to rectify it should the necessity arise.

For fear of misunderstanding it must be repeated that nothing that has been said here is intended to refer to the intelligent minority. Those who can reach a reasonable standard in three or four languages, or can assimilate a sufficiently substantial knowledge of mathematical or scientific bookwork to enable them to attack in the right way fairly advanced problems in either subject, or acquire a knowledge of history that will fit them later, if they have the time and the taste, for original research, will always be able to learn for themselves all that is necessary of anything they wish. For them the teacher is merely a convenient aid. His really important function is to educate those who cannot or will not educate themselves. It must never be forgotten that it is these last who form the bulk of public opinion and on whom the future of the country depends. The lamentable state of mind in which most of them leave school at present may be illustrated by the following scene of which one of the authors was a witness.

At the beginning of the war five Eton masters and one boy, who had just finished his Eton career and had up to then shown no special ability, went to a camp where part of the new army was being trained. The boy in question and two of the masters were joining one of the battalions there for the period of the war. The other three had been asked to come to help to look after the men while the officers were being taught their business. One day it was announced that on the following night the brigade would take part in outpost duty. The boy in question asked after dinner whether one of the masters could tell him anything about outposts. 'Look in the drill book !' came the answer in chorus, and someone found the place and handed him the book. Somewhat unwillingly he sat down, began to read, became gradually more and more engrossed, and at the end of about half an hour got up ejaculating : 'Well, this is the first time I ever realised that one could find out anything one wanted to know from a book !'

So far nothing has been said of what in most schools are treated as extra subjects for which additional fees are charged, boys having to find such opportunities as they can in their playtime for instruction in them. They comprise music, drawing and painting and other forms of art, carpentry and metal work, physical training, and, lastly, the drill required in the Officers' Training Corps for recruits and for those who take the military certificate A.

All who have had any experience of the organisation of a big public school know that the problem of dealing with these subjects is one of great complexity ; and at Eton, at any rate, no satisfactory solution of it has yet been found. Those who agree that the first essential at the present time for the improvement of the education of boys of average or rather less than average intellectual capacity is a drastic reduction of the number of subjects taught will be apt to resent the introduction into the curriculum of any extra burden. Yet nothing is more certain than that a place *must* be found for at least one of these activities during a very considerable portion of any boy's school career.

The five subjects mentioned above do not, however, fall into one category. Music, drawing, painting and the like form one class ; carpentry and metal work another ; P.T. and O.T.C. requirements a third. In the first a considerable amount of personal instruction and supervision must be given continuously. In the second, except in the earliest stages, individual practice with occasional reference to an expert is all that is needed. In the third group physical training, though beneficial, is not essential for a boy who is increasing his muscular development by a variety of forms of violent exercise ; while the requirements of the O.T.C. occupy only two periods of about two months each in a boy's school life.

In what follows, the Eton arrangement of hours is taken for the sake of illustration. The principles laid down could, however, be applied to many other schemes of work. The fact that at Eton pupil-room work bulks larger, and school hours are consequently fewer, than in most other schools probably makes the solution of the problem harder there than elsewhere.

It was suggested in Chapter IV, p. 78, that each boy should have two 8-hour subjects, including divinity and an outline of history, and two 4-hour subjects, making 24 hours (or periods) in all. But in four out of the six blocks into which the school is divided there are, as a matter of fact, twenty-five periods a week varying in length from 50 to 60 minutes. The twenty-fifth hour is a fourth morning school on Tuesdays at a time available on other days for pupil-room or extras, or, in the case of boys not required on any particular day for either, for recreation or work of their own.

It would be possible to have such a fourth morning school not on Tuesdays only, but on four days a week, counting it as something midway between extras and school, from which individual boys, wanted at certain times of the year to play in some important match, might be excused. One day would be assigned to block C, another to block D, and so on. Boys who did not wish to learn music, or drawing, or carpentry, and who were not required for any military training, would be grouped in classes for P.T. The scheme would be elastic, for there would be nothing to prevent boys in one block being grouped with boys in another block, if such an arrangement suited the O.T.C. or P.T. instructors better. Each boy would have one hour a week for the subject of his choice without any addition to his tale of school hours. The time available for this fourth school would enable music masters to give lessons to two boys in the period, so that the ten or twelve music masters available could deal with from twenty to thirty boys in each school, thus providing for the best part of a hundred pupils, which would go far to meet the demand. The transference of a pupil from a big block to a small one for this purpose would offer no difficulty.

Boys who wished to take advantage of the instruction thus given in more than one subject would probably find no difficulty in getting accommodated in the hours of some block other than their own.

The second music lesson in the week that is at present considered normal would have to come, as it does now, out of the learner's spare time ; but the provision of eight music lesson periods each week without the addition of an extra school to any individual boy would help to relieve the difficulty now experienced in finding time for music.

The details of such a scheme could be varied almost infinitely to suit different schools. The two principles underlying the idea are, firstly, that boys should be encouraged as far as possible to take up some subject that will enlarge the scope of their intellectual and artistic appreciation in later life and give the opportunity of self-expression in something that lies outside their daily work to those who have the necessary capacity ; secondly, that they cannot all attempt to get even a bowing acquaintance with more than a limited number of subjects.

It should be added that their artistic efforts need by no means be devoted solely to music or drawing. At Eton great success has attended the endeavours of those in charge of the drawing school to foster latent talent in every possible way. Leather-cutting, etching, modelling, pottery, the making of marionettes and the designing and manufacture of their dresses, are all open to any who wish to try their hand at such pastimes, and the number of those interested in one or other of them is steadily increasing. Acting, too, is now playing its part among the recreations to which boys devote some of their spare time ; and, though it is no part of the function of a public school to train boys for the stage, and the desire to appear in the limelight—literally and metaphorically—is one to be encouraged very sparingly, if at all, the performance of Shakespeare or of French plays cannot fail to give a great stimulus, literary and linguistic, to the performers, and other boys are likely to be tempted to investigate for themselves works that seem to have so much attraction for some of their companions.

That in their early stages these extra subjects had better be regarded as an interest of a lighter and more amusing type than other parts of school work will probably only be denied by a few enthusiasts who regard Art as the be-all and end-all of existence. Yet aptitude in one or two of such pursuits is becoming an increasingly practical asset as the careers selected by boys and their parents become progressively wider in range. Three-quarters of a century ago the choice of a profession was with rare exceptions limited for a boy of good family to the Navy, the Army, the Church and the Bar, or, for those born to it, a place in the family bank. The bulk of the country gentlemen drew their revenue from their rents, and their main occupation consisted in sitting on the bench of magistrates and looking after local affairs. Now, when positions in any kind of business, retail as well as wholesale, are eagerly sought after, when the laying out of gardens or golf courses, the production of manures for private lawns or potato fields, the application of scientific methods to the making of aeroplane engines or beer, the salvation of the coconut trees in the Fiji Islands or the importation of strange animals from every part of the world to the London or other Zoological Gardens, the making of carpets and cricket bats, the management of hotels or newspapers, the designing of tapestries for churches or drainage systems for the fens, when these and many other similar activities provide occupation for every class of society, it is hard to say that there is any form of human knowledge which should be excluded from the education of a great school. *Quot capitum vivunt, totidem studiorum Milia.* This very multiplicity of pursuits makes it more than ever clear that the object of a public school education must be not to impart information on a large number of subjects, but to give boys such a suppleness of brain and such a comprehension of what real knowledge implies as will fit them to deal with the innumerable problems which in this welter of possibilities may confront them throughout their career.

It has already been pointed out (Chapter II, p. 39) that the introduction of a new subject into the curriculum presents certain difficulties in connection with the status and efficiency of those employed to teach it. At Eton most of the extra subjects under discussion have for various reasons escaped these difficulties. Long before the period covered by this book the drawing master had been an Evans. The first of them was the elder Samuel. William, the second of the family to hold the post, established the boys' house destined to be known by the name of Evans' for nearly seventy years, and from 1878 to

1906 managed, single-handed, by his daughter Jane. He was himself an Old Etonian, possessed of great physical strength, and already, when he started the house, occupied a leading position in everything connected with boating and bathing. He therefore possessed in an eminent degree all the qualities then required for a master, and drawing was thus given a start vouchsafed to very few new subjects. This tradition was carried on by his son, the second Samuel, and his grandson, Sidney, the latter not resigning until 1922. When this family connection thus ceased it fortunately happened that there was already on the staff as a modern linguist an ideal successor in the person of Eric Powell, who immediately set to work greatly to extend the scope of his department. He introduced new forms of artistic activity, inaugurated a succession of exhibitions of various kinds, and by his example and his character inspired increasing enthusiasm, while mainly owing to his energy the old drawing school was replaced by a far worthier building. He subsequently succeeded to a boys' house which he rapidly made one of the best in Eton, and the loss inflicted on the school by his death in the Alps in 1933 was in many ways irremediable. From the point of view of drawing, however, the blow was rendered less serious by the fact that he had already secured the services of Frederick Menzies-Jones as his second in command, and, under the auspices of the latter and Robert Darwin, the work started nearly a century and a half ago continues with its traditional success.

Music in its present form began with the appointment of Sir Joseph Barnby in 1875. Though the College Chapel choir and the Musical Society already existed, as will appear later, it was his inspiring energy that first made them of real value to the school, and the soundness of his work is shown by the size and proficiency of the Musical Society and the high place held by the Chapel choir among the Cathedral choirs of the country. Nor is this all, for to the Musical Society has been added an orchestra composed entirely of boys, and the Chapel choir is on occasions reinforced by the choir of Lower Chapel, also drawn entirely from members of the school.

Lovers of music at Eton have exceptional privileges. In addition to frequent invitation concerts of great merit given by individuals, five subscription concerts take place yearly, and at these much of the best talent of the country is wont to appear. Nor must the excellent concerts of the Gramophone Society by any means be forgotten. But above all these must be ranked the services in the College Chapel, led by the professional choir. Their dignity and splendour are an ineffaceable memory in the minds of almost all Etonians when much else has sunk into comparative oblivion.

Throughout the seventeen years of Sir Joseph Barnby's precentorship and most of the twenty-two of his successor, Dr. C. H. Lloyd, private musical instruction was confined to out-of-school hours and suffered accordingly. But a great change was made when one out of the two half-hours assigned to private teaching in music was included within the periods of regular school. Whether this invasion of the already exiguous school hours was in all respects desirable or likely to be maintained permanently may be doubted, but its effect on music was immediate and striking. It ceased at once to be a mere 'extra', and its change of status was confirmed under Dr. Alington not only by its admission to the list of subjects for Extra Studies in A block during regular school hours, but by its addition to those covered by the inclusive fee. Thus boys can be taught music privately, and join the Musical Society, without payment of any kind. It is therefore not surprising that there are between two and three hundred boys learning to play some kind of instrument and about an equal number singing in the Musical Society, so that altogether about a third of the school is receiving musical instruction in some form.

The advance in the status of music has been carried further by the present Precentor, Dr. H. Ley, who has arranged that some of the music teachers shall no longer be mere visiting masters, but be residents, employed for their whole time, and have, so far as possible, academical qualifications equal to those of the rest of their colleagues. At the same time the standard of the choir school—part of the original foundation of the College—has been raised by association with the teaching staff of the school, and a prosperous Old Choristers' Association has come into being. In consequence the competition for entry into the choir school has grown very severe.

Music is thus in a most interesting stage. It has for some while past ceased to be the luxury of a few, and now, aided by the genius, energy and tact of the Precentor, it seems in a fair way to become an integral part of the educational structure.

Carpentry and metal work, physical training and the knowledge of drill required for the handling of a platoon or a company on parade do not present the same difficulties as more intellectual pursuits in the provision of an efficient staff of instructors. For work in wood and metal professional teaching is not hard to obtain. For physical training and drill the Navy and Army turn out a large number of men of the best type. The gymnasium was for a short time compulsory for lower boys, but is now entirely voluntary. Its management was originally in the hands of officers, but experience has shown that it can be safely entrusted to naval petty officers or military drill sergeants. Great interest is taken in the house gymnastic competition for lower boys. The school boxing arouses almost as much enthusiasm as any of the various games or athletic contests ; and the present record of the school in fencing is quite exceptional. As regards the O.T.C., an officer seconded from the regular army supervises the drilling of recruits, arranges field days and parades, and gives most of the instruction for certificate A. He is also responsible for the rifle shooting, which is carried on partly by means of a miniature range under cover, partly on the rifle range proper. All these interests have their votaries, and in the aggregate provide eminently useful occupation for a large number of boys who for one reason or another are unlikely to win distinction in the more ordinary school games.

CHAPTER VI

THE OBJECT OF EDUCATION

Dangers of diffuseness

The suggestions made in the first chapter concerning a child's early education and the age at which it should begin leads at once to the question : What is education? To this question there are, broadly speaking, two answers. Probably the more popular view is that the schoolmaster who, in his later life, sees most of his old pupils in high position has been the most successful teacher, his success being measured by the extent to which he has enabled them to climb higher than their competitors. If this is to be re-garded as the main object of education, it is best attained by following the fashion of the day. As a rule it is difficult for those who have not received a conventional education to get a start in any position likely to lead to public success. Of course there are exceptions, for there are some men of such outstand-ing qualities that under any conditions they are bound to rise, if they wish. The number of those fit for such pre-eminence is, however, strictly limited, and among them are many who in spite of their gifts have no desire for the limelight.

This answer to the question, then, at best only touches the fringe of the problem. It entirely disregards the vast majority who are not sufficiently gifted ever to aspire to distinction. Yet it is the education of this majority which is of far greater importance than that of the talented minority. The latter will always somehow manage to acquire whatever knowledge is needed. On the character of the instruction given to the former depend the reserves on which the country will have to draw in times of stress, and the attitude to education of all kinds adopted by the coming generation.

For the education of this majority there are certain essentials. The first is thoroughness. An unintellectual boy must begin by learning the meaning of knowledge. So many boys think that they know a lesson when with some difficulty and a certain amount of charity on the part of the master they can score half marks in it. Obviously, if this is all they can do five minutes after they have learnt the lesson, nothing whatever will remain in their minds a week later. To be content with a few vague scraps of information which vanish in a few hours is not only useless but positively harmful. At whatever cost of time and trouble a boy must be made to realise that he cannot be said to know anything which he is unable to reproduce promptly and accurately for at any rate several days after he has learnt it. The good teacher will be prepared to repeat the same thing, if necessary in the same form, not two or three but a dozen or more times. Against this it is sometimes argued that endless repetition bores the learner. The truth, however, is exactly the opposite. When even a minimum of knowledge and the feeling of confidence that comes with it has once been acquired, the slowest learner ceases to be bored. Of course he cannot be relieved of all drudgery, for drudgery is to some extent inherent in the earliest stages of all subjects, whatever their nature. But boys very rarely find work dull if they feel that it is leading them somewhere. What not only bores them, but causes either antagonism or despair, according to the individual character, is the subconscious conviction that they are making no progress and that all their labour is a futile waste of time.

These considerations render it essential to avoid what is becoming the chief danger of modern education—the attempt to multiply beyond the capacity of the learner the number of subjects taught. This is due partly to the tendency to frame the curriculum of a school to suit the requirements of the better boys, while the others are left to drag along behind as best they may ; partly to outside pressure from amateur educationists, who usually have a pet subject which to them is the one thing needful.

But, while it is comparatively easy to point out what to avoid, it is a very different matter to lay down what should form the common basis for early education. The necessary machinery of school life, considerations of expense, and, last but not least, the limited supply of teaching power in any but the usual standard subjects, render it impossible to offer an unlimited variety of choice.

A teacher's stock-in-trade costs time and money to

produce. Grammars, well-edited texts with the right kind of notes, collections of suitable extracts for translation at sight, books on science that a boy of moderate intelligence can understand in the early stages, mathematical examples with the necessary amount of explanation, are the accumulation of many years after a subject has come to be recognised in the curriculum of a large number of schools. Latin and Greek in this respect have the tradition of centuries behind them. French and to a lesser extent German are barely beginning to be properly equipped. Mathematicians have recast their whole system more than once during the past generation and it is doubtful if the last word has yet been said. In science the lack of clear, well-written text-books may be due to the difficulty of expressing what is wanted without the use of technical terms, but it is probable that more can be done in this direction in course of time. New life has been infused into history by the work of Messrs. Warner and Marten, but similar introductions to the development of other European nations, of the United States and of the East have still to be produced.

Moreover the staff of a big school cannot suddenly be diverted from the teaching of ancient or modern languages to that of other branches of learning. Even were it possible to dismiss half the old staff at a year's notice, a sufficiency of men possessing the requisite knowledge and also the other qualities indispensable in a schoolmaster could not be found. At Eton, for instance, when it was decided that science must form part of the ordinary school course, three or four scientists of real eminence were imported. Though they knew their subject, their failure to maintain order made science a laughing-stock among boys and masters, and reduced it to a position from which it has taken all the skill and energy of its present exponents to rescue it.

Besides these practical difficulties which the theorist is apt to forget, there is another drag on the wheels of the public schools which precludes progress as rapid as many may wish to see in the modernisation of the ordinary subjects of study. It took nearly half a century to persuade the authorities of Oxford and Cambridge to open their doors to boys who could not offer Greek. It would be rash to prophesy how many years will elapse before they act up to the name of University and put all subjects on a common footing, merely exacting a real proficiency in the groups offered by various candidates for admission. Till they do so boys at school must be taught Latin, mathematics and some modern language, besides being expected to pass, at any rate for Oxford and for the school certificate, in a paper on some English author or authors. Even those who have obtained exemption from Responsions or the Previous Examination and have begun to concentrate on other subjects are required by many colleges to pass another examination in which Latin is compulsory.

These demands make it necessary for a boy at school during the period after he has taken the school certificate examination to keep up his acquaintance with a varied assortment of subjects which he is going to drop completely as soon as he gets to the University, when he might otherwise be concentrating on a more limited range of study and laying a sound foundation in some department of knowledge likely to be of use to him both at the University and in after life.

Public schools, therefore, have not got a free hand. They are hampered at both ends. Boys come to them, as has been shown (pp. 22–24), who have been sent to their private schools too late to be got up to a satisfactory standard ; and the demands of Navy, Army and University examinations —the Air Force is omitted because it leaves its candidates a free choice—necessitate the retention in the curriculum of more subjects than it is advisable for the majority to attempt. The problem of providing the kind of education best suited to the requirements of the inconspicuous majority of learners is therefore a complex one. Reformers have to bear in mind not only what is the nearest approach to an ideal system, but also what is practicable in view of existing conditions.

From whichever angle, however, the question is approached, three cardinal propositions may be laid down, neglect of which will wreck almost any scheme. In the first place the number of subjects taught must be kept within reasonable limits ; the average boy's mind cannot grapple with more than four, or at the very outside five, simultaneously. Secondly, it must be remembered that the basis of all early education must be linguistic or literary—preferably a combination of the two. Lastly, it is impossible to get the best results unless the learner believes that the knowledge he is being made to acquire has some ultimate value to him. This does not mean that all teaching is to be conducted on the line of least resistance. Every subject, if properly handled, contains quite enough material to train the beginner's mind in the art of concentration on points not intrinsically interesting to him.

For boys of more than average capacity there are probably no subjects combining both the literary and the linguistic qualities required that can be compared with Greek and Latin. No living language can be reduced to such a completely classified system of grammatical rules, and at the same time their literature is superb. But the attempt that has been widely made to keep Latin and drop Greek is a failure; and the rarer effort to save Greek by dropping Latin is still less successful. Wedded to one another, each forms the other's complement. Divorced, each lacks what only the other can give. It is not merely that Latin is the more exact, the more matter-of-fact, the more prosaic language, Greek the livelier, the more untrammelled. There is another, more technical reason. It does not take a moderately sensible pupil very long to get to the point in Latin when he can without much mental effort make out the simpler portions of Cæsar, Cornelius Nepos and even Ovid. What is to happen then? In Latin the next stage is singularly poor. There is plenty of

Cicero that is not very hard to translate, but most of it deals with abstract questions of a kind entirely foreign to the youthful intelligence. There are, too, plenty of authors whose subject-matter is often almost thrillingly interesting—Tacitus, Juvenal, some of Cicero's speeches, Horace, parts of Virgil, Plautus, Lucan. But the style of these and other similar authors is such that their language is almost incomprehensible to ordinary boys of fifteen or sixteen. There is remarkably little Latin interesting in matter and moderately simple in manner ; and the ordinary boy has to be confined to a rather monotonous round, or else to read extracts taken out of their setting and therefore robbed of much of their literary value.

Latin, moreover, bristles with allusions to incidents in Greek history and tales drawn from Greek mythology. This would not matter so much if time could be found for consecutive instruction in these subjects ; but the pressure that has to such a large extent driven Greek out of the modern curriculum has also taken away the hours available for such teaching. The average boy cannot make much progress in Latin without a considerable amount of instruction each week in grammar, translation at sight and composition. For the first it is essential that he should be tested both in the knowledge of his rules and also, by means of short sentences, in their application. The other two require at least one school apiece in which he may write his translation from Latin into English or from English into Latin. At least one more hour is needed in which the master, having corrected the boy's attempts, can go through the exercises and point out the right way of dealing with difficulties. For all this four or five hours a week are barely sufficient, and another hour of the boy's time is required for the preparation of the grammar lesson or lessons. Nor do boys of the type in question automatically pick up much vocabulary. They must be made to learn lists of words and phrases, which want pretty constant revision ; as, too, do the grammatical rules learnt each week. If the time spent in reading a reasonable amount of prose and poetry is also taken into account, it will be seen that a total of seven or eight hours a week is the bare minimum required to give such boys confidence in their own capacity and stimulate their interest. Any system that fails to do this is worse than useless. The boy, imbued with the belief that he is constitutionally stupid and cannot hope to succeed, gradually drifts into the ranks of the class, far too numerous at most public schools, that has ceased to have any intellectual interest, content to scrape through its lessons anyhow and resignedly to do the punishments incurred, when the work produced falls below some ridiculously low pass standard. All attempt at concentration vanishes. School is regarded as a necessary evil to be got through with the smallest possible amount of effort ; and conscience and pride are mollified by the reflection that after all Latin is only a musty old dead language which no one wants to learn and which will never be touched again when school days are over.

What is true of the time required to make Latin of real educational value for the kind of boy under discussion is true in a minor degree of other subjects. The necessary minimum varies according to the ramifications and difficulty of each ; but the slow learner will get little good out of any subject to which he does not devote at least four or five hours weekly. Where then is the time to be found for six or seven ? They involve from thirty-five to forty hours a week—six or seven a day—in school, without counting the time spent by the boy in preparing his work. It is the failure to recognise this elementary principle that makes it possible for boys who have been doing Latin for seven or eight years to know nothing of the Latin for the four ordinary points of the compass, of the Roman method of reckoning dates, of what was happening in Italy during the life-time of Our Lord ; that makes them confuse the three fates with the Gorgons ; or think that *loci* is the plural of locust.

For such boys, then, either Latin must be discarded ; or, if the University authorities insist on it in their entrance examinations, it must be treated as a mere 'cram' subject of no educational value ; or, thirdly, it must be given seven or eight hours a week, and not more than three other subjects must be attempted. One of these must then obviously be mathematics, for some familiarity with figures is necessary in every walk of life. How far this should be carried must, however, depend on the individual. Public opinion will hardly permit of the complete omission of modern languages, so French seems bound to have a place. The choice of the fourth subject is to some extent limited by the number of properly qualified teachers available—of which something is said elsewhere—and lies, as a rule, between another modern language, history and some form of science.

Of modern languages Spanish and Italian have so much in common with French and Latin, and yet so many differences, that it is confusing to begin the three simultaneously. Indeed, the general consensus of opinion among those who have tried to teach languages is that a third should not be taken till at least one of the others is comparatively well known. On the principle already enunciated, that the basis of all education must be literary or linguistic—and, if possible, both—history is to be preferred to science ; and it has the additional advantage of lending itself to instruction in the art of writing clear, grammatical English and arranging facts and ideas in their proper sequence.

Such then, if Latin is to be retained, seems to be the almost inevitable curriculum for boys of moderate or meagre ability. But it has one great defect. It has already been pointed out that Latin is deficient in literature of the medium kind of difficulty—something midway between Cæsar and Tacitus, between Æsop's Fables and the bulk of Ovid or Virgil. In French, too, once the initial stages are past, translation into schoolboy English becomes a mere matter of vocabulary, while in history a little capacity for writing round any topic and hanging a multitude of words on a few pegs of knowledge enables the writer to reach some sort of pass standard without much application. In this curriculum, therefore, no subject but mathematics necessitates real concentration beyond the first year or two. But without concentration the thoroughness that has been postulated above as the first essential of education is unattainable.

It was in this respect that Greek played such an important part in the old wholly classical education. The boy who had got past the most elementary stage in Latin was faced with a new script, new declensions, new conjugations. He could not even read a line of his book without giving all his attention to the task. This effort was invaluable. But the devotion of eight or nine years to the attainment of a mediocre knowledge of two dead languages was a palpable waste of time, and left the victim so ill equipped with practical information, that such a system could not survive when life became more difficult and the competition for employment more intense.

Unluckily the struggle between the old order and the new, between a purely classical education and one that embraced more generally useful knowledge, developed into a struggle for the retention or abolition of Greek as a necessary test at the Universities, and the real problem was hopelessly obscured. The question is not whether Latin and Greek provide a good medium of intellectual development. No unbiassed observer can doubt that for those who have really learnt them they have done all that any form of education obtainable at school can be expected to do. But scholars of this class are among the gifted few to whom the acquisition of almost any kind of knowledge comes easily. The sufficiency of the classics in their case is no argument for ignoring the needs of those who, for one cause or another, have spent years without succeeding in learning enough of them to write half a dozen lines of either Greek or Latin correctly, or to read the literature of either intelligently. To expect that the latent powers of these weaker vessels will be brought out by a prolonged course of the mental pabulum that they have proved unable to digest, is as sensible as to expect the health of a child with a delicate stomach to be improved by a prolonged diet of beef and beer ; while the wisdom of retaining one of the two offending articles of consumption is on a par with that of a doctor who should recommend his patient to drop the beef, but to peg away at the beer, or *vice versa*.

It remains then to prescribe the diet that will provide the necessary nutrition to the less sturdy mind without cloying it. The case for a reduction in the demands made on the mental digestion has already been stated, and the claims of French, history and—up to a point—mathematics have been advanced. A fourth subject is required that will at a fairly early stage provide the necessary stimulus to concentration without revolting the intellectual stomach as Latin has in so many cases been found to do. The desiderata are a script that it takes an effort to read, a new accidence to be learnt, and a literature that contains a sufficiency of attractive matter expressed in moderately simple language. A case could no doubt be made out for several eastern languages—especially, among English boys, for one of those current in India. But no one with any experience of English schoolboys can have much doubt as to the kind of reception that might be expected by the rash moonshee who should venture to instruct a division of average Etonians or Harrovians in Hindustani, Tamil or Urdu. For the time being a less ambitious programme must suffice.

Of European languages, with the possible exception of Russian, German is the only one that fulfils the required conditions. It has a script of its own, which, though now not essential, should certainly be mastered by beginners for the reasons given above ; its nouns, adjectives and verbs are very largely inflected ; and it has a considerable amount of literature of a character likely to be attractive to young minds and not difficult in form. Unlike the Romance languages, in which the advanced stages are the hardest to master, German resembles Greek in the fact that the chief struggle comes early and that once the elements of the grammar are grasped the satisfying consciousness of rather rapid progress is not long delayed.

The omission of English from this curriculum is not due to disbelief in its importance. It has been said in Chapter I that a boy must be taught in the very earliest stages to understand clearly the structure of an English sentence. This should be begun even before he goes to a preparatory school. Once he has acquired the elementary principles of the language, formal lessons in English cease to be of much value. His knowledge of it will be fostered by translation from other languages, if this is properly taught. There is no better training in English than the struggle to render the idioms of Latin, French or German into the corresponding idoms of the mother tongue, while the insight gained into the exact meaning of an English author in the attempt to render that meaning into another language is no less valuable. For original composition history offers unlimited opportunities. The study of English as a language should go hand in hand with the study of every other department of the boy's work.

Geography, too, is intentionally not counted as a separate subject. A rough outline of most countries is soon learnt. The basis of further geographical knowledge should be historical, showing how natural causes led to the development of particular towns ; what physical features have affected the progress of different countries ; what barriers have had to be overcome in various campaigns. Bicycles and motor-cars teach most boys map-reading, and if, in addition, the habit of looking on a map as the ordinary way of ascertaining the relative position of different places is acquired, further instruction in geography is superfluous. That a wide educational structure might be based on geography alone is not denied. But at present lack of teachers and the demands of examinations make this impracticable.

CHAPTER VII

FROM DAMES AND DOMINES TO MASTERS

The development of Boarding Houses

The boarding of boys at Eton was not until comparatively recently a matter of concern to the authorities of the school. Maxwell Lyte in his *History of Eton College* says that in 1766 'for some 450 Oppidans there were thirteen boarding-houses of which three were kept by men commonly styled "domines", and the remainder by "dames" of the opposite sex.' Later evidence seems to show that the houses must have been smaller and more numerous than this, but the principle remains that they were kept by people who had no official connection with the school, and that anyone who could attract customers might try his or her hand at the business. Little by little, however, it occurred to the assistant masters that it was not beneath their dignity to add to their incomes by taking in boarders, for in another place Maxwell-Lyte says : 'There is apparently no record of the exact date at which the Assistant Masters entered into competition with the "Domines" or "Dames" by establishing boarding-houses for their respective pupils. . . . George Heath is said to have received pupils before his election to the Head Mastership', which he held from 1792 to 1802. So, apparently, did W. H. Roberts before he was made a Fellow and Bursar in 1771.[1] It therefore seems possible that by about the end of the eighteenth century tutors' houses began to compete with those of dames. As the tutors were his assistants the Headmaster had some authority over their arrangements, and apparently early in the last century he limited numbers in the tutors' houses, but in compensation allowed a higher fee to be charged. By the middle of the nineteenth century the Headmaster began to have some control over the succession to 'dames' houses, but never over the number of boys they might receive.

The next stage was marked by the appearance of assistant masters who were not tutors, as holders of boarding houses. About 1858 Dr. Goodford improved the position of the assistants in the mathematical school 'by the concession to them of the right to wear academical costume in church and in school. Some of them also received permission to keep boarding houses, though not invested with the disciplinary authority of the regular Assistant Masters, and regarded as "Dames", or more strictly "Domines"' (Maxwell-Lyte). Thus was introduced the word 'dame' in the sense in which it was used through the latter half of the nineteenth century, to denote the holder of a boarding house who taught any subject other than classics.

Writing of Dr. Hornby's headmastership, Maxwell Lyte notes—

[1] *Etoniana*, R. A. Austen-Leigh, No. 15.

'a rise in the status of the teachers [of mathematics] who, from being merely Assistants to the Mathematical Master, became Assistants to the Head Master. The teachers of Mathematics, of French, and of physical science, are now on the same footing as the teachers of Latin or Greek, exercising authority out of school as well as in school. They have gradually supplanted the "Dames" in the boarding houses, the College refusing to renew leases of such houses to persons of either sex not belonging to the educational staff.'

Of this process of systematisation, consolidation and equalisation of houses a few details may now be given.

In 1868 there were 796 Oppidans in

2 houses containing	50 boys or more
2 ,,	,, 40–49 ,,
10 ,,	,, 30–39 ,,
6 ,,	,, 20–29 ,,
6 ,,	,, 10–19 ,,
3 ,,	,, 5–9 ,,
3 ,,	,, 1–4 ,,

Total number of houses, 32.

In addition there were 6 home boarders or day boys.

Of the holders of houses three were ladies, and of the male 'dames' one was a Conduct, one a drawing —that is to say extra—master, four were mathematical or science masters, and two had no teaching post at all.

In 1883, Dr. Hornby's last summer Half, 833 Oppidans were distributed in 29 houses thus :

4 houses containing 40–49 boys
15   ,,   ,,   30–39 ,,
2   ,,   ,,   20–29 ,,
4   ,,   ,,   10–19 ,,
3   ,,   ,,   5–9 ,,
1   ,,   ,,   1–4 ,,

Of the 'dames' one was a lady, one a Conduct, the remaining eight regular mathematical, science or language masters.

By 1897 the same process had gone further, for the number of Oppidans had risen to 955, while that of houses had fallen to 27, the distribution of boys being as follows :

In 1 house containing 50 boys
,, 3 houses   ,,   40 ,,
,, 20   ,,   ,, 30–39 ,,
,, 3   ,,   ,, 10–19 ,,

There were four home boys in addition to the above.

Of the houses not held by classical tutors one—the largest—was managed by Miss Evans,[1] nine were in the hands of regular non-classical masters.

In 1910 the plan had become much simpler. There were eleven houses containing forty boys or more, fourteen with from thirty to forty, one 'holding house' with five, twenty-six houses thus accommodating 948 Oppidans. The only real 'dame' had by then disappeared, and eleven houses were held by non-classical masters.

[1] See Chapter V, pp. 105–6.

About this period a line of policy adopted some time previously by the College began to make itself felt. Originally houses had been built and equipped by the private enterprise of individuals. In consequence many of the buildings, not intended in the first instance to last long, were rapidly falling out of repair, and, being in private ownership, could not be satisfactorily dealt with. The College therefore, as opportunity offered, set to work to acquire all boarding houses, letting them to masters at a reasonable rent and itself undertaking all structural repairs and improvements. This secured economy in upkeep and saved masters the anxiety of having to purchase their houses. At the time of writing all houses but one are owned by College.

During and after the war no great change occurred in the grouping of houses ; in fact the only alteration up to the present has been a general increase in size owing to the growth of the school.

In 1936 about 1,080 Oppidans were distributed thus :

  In 8 houses containing 45–49 boys
  ,, 12 ,,   ,, 40–44 ,,
  ,, 5   ,,   ,, 35–39 ,,
  ,, 1 'holding house' with about 10.

Non-classical housemasters number 14, thus being, at any rate temporarily, in a majority.

It is to be hoped that a new building programme now in its early stages will enable the size of existing houses to be gradually reduced. There is little doubt that under present conditions at Eton the ideal number of boys for one house is round about forty, not more.

From what has been said it will be apparent that just after the middle of the nineteenth century the house was still a private enterprise, its success or failure depending on the quality of the master and of the boys he attracted. As the house grew in numbers, master and boys moved from building to building and only came to rest with the occupation of one of the larger houses. On the master's retirement his house was broken up, many of the older boys left, the others had to find shelter where they could, and the progress from building to building began afresh. The system was wasteful, for few housemasters during a normally successful career escaped with less than three moves, and some suffered considerably more. Also the contrast between house and house was unavoidably great and, incidentally, this made athletic competitions between houses on anything like equal terms impossible. But, as in most forms of individualism, the battle really did go to the strong, and the weak, perhaps deservedly, went to the wall, and some of their boys with them.

By the outset of the twentieth century, owing to the elimination of the smaller house and the approach to equalisation of the rest, it became possible to keep the boys in a house together after the departure of the master. His successor was able to take over all boys who remained at Eton, but usually had to move them to another smaller or less attractive building.

Thus changes from building to building, though less frequent, are still necessary, and will be finally got rid of only when the size and amenities of buildings have become approximately equal. Then, perhaps, when a master retires his boys will not have to move, and he alone will be replaced. Thus the traditions of the house will tend to centre more round the building and less round the house-tutor. Such a system would no doubt be more economical; but if, as seems possible, its advantages involve the loss of some of the tutor's personal influence, the loss will exceed the gain.

As to the succession of masters to houses, from the moment when regular masters of the school began to take boarders there was theoretically no doubt of the position of the Headmaster. He could grant or refuse permission to a master to take a boarding house and could regulate as might seem best to him length and conditions of tenure. But so long as houses were built, equipped, or purchased by an enterprising master out of his own pocket, it was in practice all but impossible to gainsay anyone anxious to make the venture, or to dislodge him when it had been made. Thus up to the end of Dr. Lyttelton's headmastership (1916) masters succeeded to houses in order of seniority almost as a matter of course, those few who were manifestly unfit usually finding another profession before their turn came. The tenure of houses was, moreover, long; for, the staff being small, a master in Dr. Hornby's day might obtain a house after from two to three years' service, and, if successful, would almost certainly remain a housemaster till his retirement, thus holding the position for thirty years or more.

The Headmaster had, therefore, to make appointments with this contingency in view ; but as the qualities of a good teacher and of a good housemaster are by no means always to be found combined in one individual, he had difficulty in finding the right men. Sometimes the teaching suffered, sometimes the house ; but on the whole the teaching, as the less important, tended to get the worst of the bargain.

A good teacher may be a man of one subject alone, and even if he has outside interests they must take second place. He has to lead, not follow, and he must not only stick to the point at the moment, but come back to it again and again, until he can be sure that it has been grasped. But the attitude of the efficient housemaster is fundamentally different. In the rush of general management, correspondence, visits from parents, and almost incessant association with boys on Sundays and weekdays alike, no single subject can ever be paramount. When he walks round his house the more diffuse he is the better. One of the authors had an experience which serves to illustrate this, and, as it was the occasion of his being paid his one and only compliment during a long life, there may be some excuse for relating it. After dining in Hall at an Oxford College he left the High Table and was passing into the outer darkness when a former pupil darted forth from the shadows. 'May I ask you a question ?' The opening was familiar enough, the question itself perhaps less so. 'Are you still ready every evening at no notice at all to say something interesting about any subject one of us chooses to start?' When the confusion of the moment was over and there had been a little time for thought, the writer remembered how often he had gone into a boy's room weary at the end of a long day and been greeted by some quite young and inconspicuous member of the house with an animated discourse on some unexpected subject which the boy had made his own and on which he was almost a specialist. Boys learn from their housemaster, but he can also learn something from them.

It must be remembered that this close relationship between boys and masters would be difficult, if not impossible, without the system of separate rooms. One of the debts which Eton owes to the seemingly fortuitous development of its Oppidan houses has been that almost from the beginning of the nineteenth century each boy has had his own room, while the only dormitory which ever existed— College Long Chamber—was abolished by 1850. To this arrangement more perhaps than to any other single factor are due certain peculiarities which distinguish Eton from many other schools where the medieval dormitory system still lingers.

With the increase in the staff during and after Dr. Warre's headmastership [1] masters had to wait longer and longer before succeeding to a house, until shortly after the war the Provost and Fellows,

[1] See p. 41.

at the instance of Dr. Alington, limited the tenure of
a house to fifteen years. Rearrangement of salaries
also made it easier for the Headmaster to exercise
his right of selection. But, even so, as long as
multiplicity of subjects renders a large staff inevitable, all masters cannot expect to become housemasters, a fact which the present Headmaster has
definitely recognised. It is evident, therefore, that
Eton masterships, which during the nineteenth
century had grown to be almost synonymous with
housemasterships, will to some extent alter in
character. The newly appointed master will no
longer be proudly conscious that in his knapsack he
carries the Field Marshal's baton, and it will not
be necessary to make appointments depend on the
probable fitness of the candidate eventually to take
a boarding house.

This change may incidentally bring with it certain
other advantages. It will be possible to appoint
men between thirty and forty years old who have
proved their capacity elsewhere. Their experience
will help to maintain a high standard of teaching.
At the same time the number of masters who are
candidates for houses will be diminished, and in
time this will accelerate promotion to houses and
so secure a longer tenure and a larger proportion
of comparatively young housemasters. It is obviously not in the best interests of the school that
no one should succeed to a house before forty—a
state of affairs which was recently only too likely to
become the general rule. After thirty the sooner a

future housemaster gets his house and the longer he keeps it the better. It cannot be right for a man to wait before entering upon what is to be his real life's work—especially when that work deals with high-spirited boys and is of the most exacting nature—till a time when the body is past its prime, and ideas and prejudices are beginning to become more rigid. This process, arrested or postponed by contact with the vigorous young life that surrounds the housemaster, may be accelerated by the drudgery of mere school work if unrelieved by any more enlivening influences. On the other hand a housemaster's task becomes easier and easier as time goes on and as he himself becomes more and more of an institution so that his actions and reactions can be relied on. Besides this, the old-established house acquires a tradition and an *esprit de corps* which are invaluable. It has to be remembered that for the first two or three years the master who is taking over someone else's boys labours in his dealings with them under the disadvantages common to all newcomers. Then again, at the end of his tenure, he cannot avoid the feeling that he will not be responsible for the most important part of the school career of the lower part of his house. Consequently, when all the necessary subtractions have been made, it will be found that the master whose time in a house is limited to fifteen or sixteen years does not enjoy his position effectively for much more than ten. The limitation to fifteen years was a measure designed to meet an unprecedented situation. It is to be hoped that the extension of this

period by one year that has just been made may
prove to be but the first step towards something more
nearly approaching the old state of affairs.

From time to time adverse comment has been made
—by the general public more often than by those
who know the system from inside—on a method of
administration which encourages or compels schoolmasters to 'keep hotels'. Critics are probably unaware of two facts : firstly, that but for the enterprise
of individuals in the late eighteenth and early
nineteenth centuries the authorities would have been
obliged to build their own barracks and the whole
history of non-local schools would have been widely
different from what it most fortunately has been ;
and, secondly, that in times of stress the modern
housemaster stands as a bulwark between the central
treasury and disaster. During the early years of the
present century prices were gradually rising, and
with the war came a rapid acceleration of this process.
In addition to this, the maintenance of a boy at
school now involves items which did not appear
earlier, such as the substitution of electric light for
the old candle and the provision of a full breakfast
instead of the former 'orders'—or ration—of bread,
butter, tea, sugar and milk. Although fees have
been raised once or twice in consequence, there has
always been a considerable 'time lag' ; that is to say,
several years have elapsed before the central authority
has been made aware of the position and has begun
to deal with it ; and even then, as an increase of
fees can only be made to apply to newcomers, three

or four more years must pass before the situation is wholly rectified. An extreme instance of this occurred after 1914. During practically the whole of the war housemasters bore all the extra expense. Then at last a request (which met with a ready response) was made to parents for a contribution to the increased cost of food; but for three or four years longer the rise in price of all other items still fell upon the housemaster.

The limitation of the period for which a master may hold a house, which was the result of the growth of the staff and consequent increase of efficiency, means further that he has fewer years in which to save enough to live on after retirement, and this retirement takes place at an earlier age. It is clear, therefore, that, collectively, housemasters have saved the central authorities a very considerable portion of the financial losses involved by the war. Supposing the much maligned 'hotel system' had not been in force, the Provost and Fellows both before, during, and after the war would have been faced with the alternatives either of raising the fees, step by step, to a figure far above their present level, or of allowing the standard of teaching and upkeep to be gravely impaired. In the former case the parents would have suffered, in the latter their boys as well.

This financial independence of the housemaster is due to the manner in which the house system originated. Though accidental it has had excellent results. It attracts the type of man fit for and ready to assume responsibility, and such men, who at many other schools would leave early in order to take some minor headmastership, find that as housemasters they have the required scope. Each housemaster rules a little kingdom of his own and in it exercises most of the functions which elsewhere fall upon the Headmaster. He settles what boys he will take in his house, the only check upon his choice being the entrance examination. His advice is frequently asked and accepted by parents when selecting a preparatory school for their boy. He conducts all correspondence ; all school reports are sent to him, and he forwards them to the parents with a covering letter giving his own views. So long as he does not contravene any rule made by the Headmaster for the whole school he is free to manage his house in his own way. All complaints from other masters are brought to him, and in the case of a breach of school rules or serious offences it rests with him whether the matter is brought before the Headmaster—or where Lower Boys are concerned the Lower Master—or not. If a boy in his house is consistently unsatisfactory, it is possible for him, without reference to anybody else, to arrange with the parents that their son shall not return to the school after the holidays. Naturally the wise housemaster, knowing what the experience of the Headmaster must be and valuing his advice, nearly always consults him unofficially in such cases. But he is not bound to do so, and in certain cases may prefer to keep his own counsel. Conversely, if a parent writes to the Headmaster about any matter concerning his boy, the Headmaster's first step is almost invariably to discuss the question with the housemaster before taking any action.

As with the position of the housemaster in his relation to the Headmaster and the school at large, so with the internal organisation of the house, development was gradual. Long before the time with which this book deals it seems to have been the custom for each house to have a captain, who was the top boy of the house in the school list and was to some extent supposed to be responsible for law and order. For instance, in the list of the captains of the house given in Major Gambier-Parry's *Annals of an Eton House* the first captain of Evans' dates back to 1839. It was, moreover, William Evans' action in building in 1855 a special room in his house for a well-stocked house library that led to the modern system of having a kind of committee of the more influential boys in the house to assist the captain in maintaining discipline. It was not, however, till towards the close of the century that this example was followed—at first by no means universally. Nowadays in boyish language 'The Library' denotes this committee of roughly half a dozen boys, and, though in the room they use there is generally a collection of books for the use of the house, this is no longer an essential.

For the administration of the everyday life of the house apart from work the boys have developed a fairly complete organisation. For the maintenance of discipline the chief authority is the captain of the house, who now has the support of the library, but in earlier days had to act alone. Football, cricket and rowing used to be looked after by the senior representative of each pursuit, but in the Easter Half there were no organised games and no one whose business it was to see that boys made reasonable use of their spare time. Gradually, however, the captain of football has come to exercise a kind of general supervision over all the usual games and sports in which the house is represented, except for cricket and rowing, which continue to be managed separately. In this capacity he is called captain of games. Naturally he acquires very nearly if not quite as much influence as the captain of the house, and it is of the utmost importance that the two should work in harmony. Of course there is nothing to prevent the same boy from acting in two or three of the capacities mentioned. In most houses the library, including the above-named officials, have a room allotted to them where they can sit and work or read.

Besides these senior boys, others reach positions of minor importance at various stages in their career. There are captains of the second football eleven, known as the 'Second Sine',[1] of the lower boy football and the 'Under Fourteen and a Half' football sides. Similarly in cricket there is a captain of the junior eleven, while on the river any member of the Boats may be called on to coach some junior crew.

Older than any of these social institutions is

[1] See p. 229.

the system of fagging. For more than a century this system has been much criticised. It has been said that it leads to much oppression of the weak by the strong ; in other words, that it encourages bullying. Maxwell-Lyte, for instance, quoting an Old Etonian's account of his time at Eton in 1824, writes : 'The condition of a junior Colleger's life at that period was very hard indeed. The practice of fagging had become an organised system of brutality and cruelty.' More than one of the Public Schools Commissioners asked questions obviously intended to elicit evidence to prove that fagging ought to be abolished. But by that time many of the worst features of the system had disappeared. Those that remained were due not to fagging in itself, but to faulty organisation. To take one example, boys got up at seven, but it was possible for a fag not to get his breakfast till ten, since no breakfast was ready for boys till nine, and the next hour was divided between fagging and pupil-room. Why breakfast could not have been ready an hour earlier is not obvious. In Dr. Hornby's day this absurdity had come to an end, though even at a later date an inconsiderate fagmaster might unduly curtail the time available for his fag's meal. This kind of fagging was, however, abolished about forty years ago by the institution of a common breakfast in each house.

No one will deny that cases of bullying may arise in connection with fagging ; but that it is not the fagging that is responsible for this is obvious from the fact that the same difficulty exists where there is no fagging ; and, if public opinion is properly guided, fagging makes it not more but less probable that anything of the sort will go on. The diametrically opposite points of view taken about the whole of this question are due to a fundamental difference of opinion as to the principles on which education—apart from instruction—should be based. It is a question between discipline and self-expression. One section of society holds that in any organised community the former must take the first place, while their opponents say that nothing but the latter is of real importance. The extremists on both sides forget that there is such a thing as ordered liberty. The boys who are sent to the bigger public schools come of a class which, as a rule, does not lack opportunities of self-expression, but owing to the superabundant vitality of young animals, which makes puppies riotous and kittens mischievous, they mostly need a considerable amount of discipline. Fagging is only a means of giving to the older and more responsible boys some share in the training of their juniors. That the power thus entrusted to them has been exercised wisely and for the general good is proved by innumerable instances within the experience of housemasters and Old Etonians. The benefit is shared equally by both fag and fagmaster ; for, if the one learns to obey, the other usually acquires the no less valuable art of exercising with restraint and tact whatever authority he may subsequently be called upon to wield.

Nothing has so far been said of the methods of dealing with illness. It should be remembered that the system of separate rooms renders the problem different from what it is elsewhere, and in the case of minor ailments easier of solution.

In schools where the boys sleep in dormitories, or some modification of them, directly a boy is ill he is taken away to the sanatorium. At Eton he remains in his own room and a label is put on his door forbidding other boys to go in. In every house there are also two or three rooms available for cases in which it is desirable to keep a boy away from the noise inseparable from the routine of a houseful of boys.

There is no special school doctor, but the parents and the housemaster between them settle whose patient among the local practitioners a boy shall be. These doctors form a medical board. This was originally appointed by Dr. Warre to advise him. Under his successors it was arranged that every doctor who had a patient in the school should be a member of this board and that a periodical report should be sent to the Headmaster for submission to the Provost and Fellows. At present the board consists of seven members.

It follows from what has been said that there is no need of a large sanatorium, and the Eton sanatorium has only twenty ordinary beds and two for scarlet fever. It contains, however, an excellent small operating theatre always ready at short notice, so that almost any surgical emergency can be dealt with on the spot. The permanent staff consists of a matron and two nurses.

If the parents prefer it, or if the sanatorium is full of infectious disease and a surgical emergency arises in the case of a non-immune subject, or if a boy sustains a fracture which needs repeated X-ray examination, he can be sent either to the Windsor Hospital or the Princess Christian's Nursing Home.

Probably the most important advantage of Eton in matters of health is that every case of illness can be and is nursed in a separate room. No doubt to this fact is owed the comparative infrequency of serious complications in epidemic diseases. It is true that the system adds greatly to the work of doctors and dames and the number of nurses at times required, but the benefits of the arrangement more than compensate for its disadvantages.

CHAPTER VIII

THE TUTORIAL SYSTEM

An Eton Speciality

The system which requires that every boy should have a master assigned to him as his more or less permanent tutor is one which, if not peculiar to Eton, is more highly developed there than at any other school. Like many other features of Eton life this system seems to have arisen naturally and almost accidentally. In early days it was no uncommon thing for the sons of the great to bring with them to school a private tutor of their own, who, like the *pædagogus* of the ancient Romans, helped them with their work and no doubt supervised their conduct. Subsequently junior masters were to some extent put in charge of the houses in which 'dames' lodged and boarded boys who came to Eton. By the beginning of the nineteenth century, and probably earlier, it had become an established custom for all boys to go to some master to get helped in their work. Payment for this work was in some cases ten, in others twenty guineas a year. William Johnson, giving evidence before the Royal Commission on Public Schools in 1862, in reply to a question about this payment describes the gradual growth of the existing arrangement :

'I can only give you', he says, 'an historical explanation of it. In the early part of the century, when there were a great number of pupils in the school, and very few masters, the assistant masters were only required to help them in construing their lessons for school, and in comparing' [composing? or preparing?] 'and looking over their exercises. There were no Sunday instruction or extra reading at all, except for individual boys. We read in the Life of Lord Metcalfe that when he was at Eton he read extra lessons in Xenophon with his tutor, who was paid, I suppose, ten guineas a year for that extra teaching. When it began to be seen that boys were required to be taught Attic Greek as well as Homeric Greek it was found not only necessary to teach one or two, such as Lord Metcalfe, but the whole of the upper classes, in matters which the school did not then teach, such as writing Greek iambics, and so on, consequently there grew up a class of private business, and extra lessons. It is not voluntary or, strictly speaking, private teaching, but still it is not what you would call the tutor's regular work; it is something in addition to the school work, and it was, generally speaking, thought that a boy ought to begin learning it when he got into the fifth form. Then men began to see that there was no reason why they should not give all the boys religious instruction on Sundays, whether they paid twenty guineas or ten. I was myself at Eton for three years without getting any religious teaching, but afterwards I had that advantage; and when I came to join the class which read Greek plays with my tutor, I had to pay ten guineas extra.'

In reply to further questions he makes it clear that the amount of this extra teaching given depends on the tutor and the amount paid for it on the parent.

'I simply leave it to the parents. I do not know why Sir S. Northcote pays twenty guineas for his boy. I take simply what is given to me. I do not receive any directions as to the private tuition or extra payment from the parents. I leave that to the dame to settle with the parents. I make no charge whatever, but simply receive what is paid to me.'

Naturally such a haphazard arrangement as to payment was bound to come to an end pretty soon ; but the amount and nature of the instruction given still remains to some extent a matter to be settled by each individual tutor, though a certain minimum has been established by custom, if not by law.

Dr. Balston, who was Headmaster in 1864 when the report of the Public Schools Commission was issued, was a strong upholder of the traditional system of education, and, in spite of the various recommendations and criticisms in respect of the Eton curriculum, hardly any changes were made up to 1868, when he resigned. The circumstances in which he had been appointed Headmaster no doubt helped to make him unwilling to initiate reforms of a drastic kind. He had had a successful career as as assistant master and had retired and taken a Fellowship shortly before his predecessor, Dr. Goodford, had been made Provost. As there was no obvious successor, Dr. Balston was persuaded to become Headmaster. But he had not sought this position and regarded himself as somewhat in the nature of a stop-gap. When it became certain that radical alterations were inevitable, he preferred to leave to another the task of making them.

Dr. Hornby took his place and, as mentioned in Chapter II, immediately began to redress the balance between pupil-room and school work. Before his time every boy in Fifth Form had to do weekly what was known as a 'Theme'—an original Latin essay on some set subject. This the tutor was required to look over carefully, turning faulty passages into Ciceronian Latin. Six or eight hours a week is the estimate of the time occupied in correcting these themes given by one of the masters examined before the Public Schools Commission.

Hornby's first step in the direction of reform was the abolition of this piece of pupil-room work and the substitution of a passage of English prose to be translated into Latin in school and looked over by the division master. He thus freed the tutor of the task of looking over these themes and returning them to the boys, which had occupied much of the period between breakfast and eleven o'clock school, and put on an additional school at 9.45 on half-holidays. He also cancelled the rule which previously compelled boys to attend Chapel every half-holiday afternoon, and got permission to institute the short morning service still in force.

The numerous other changes for the better of which he was the author did not affect the work of boys and masters in pupil-room, the amount of which was still enormous. It is true that he gave tutors the option of substituting Latin prose for the weekly Latin verses for boys who had reached Upper Division ; but this did not make much difference, as the length of this prose exercise was such as to make its correction almost as laborious as that of the previous copy of verses.

Those accustomed to the curriculum of the present day will not fully realise what pupil-room work meant unless they bear in mind that, when Dr. Warre succeeded Dr. Hornby in 1884, one lesson a week had to be construed in pupil-room by all boys in Upper Division ; seven lessons by Middle Division and Lower Division ; six by Remove ; and three by Fourth Form. Every Greek construe entailed, besides, the looking over of 'derivations —a set of twelve Greek verbs out of the lesson, of which each boy had to write out the parsing and principal parts, showing them up in school with the tutor's signature and corrections. Greek composition—prose or verse— was also looked over and emended by the tutor. Latin verses were a further complication. It was the fashion for each division master to set between twenty and thirty lines of English poetry to be turned into Latin verse, or occasionally a subject on which the boys had to write a Latin poem of their own, so that the unlucky tutor had to correct often as many as a dozen different copies.

The only thing that made it possible for the tutor to cope with all this was the small amount of work to be done for school. Fifth Form masters were in school only fifteen hours a week, and rarely had to look over anything but answers to Sunday and History Questions and a piece of Latin prose.

But how such a mass of pupil-room work was dealt with by those appointed before 1860, who frequently took fifty or sixty pupils and in some cases grappled with over seventy, is a mystery. It was shown by the evidence given before the Commissioners that on ordinary whole schooldays men who did so had to work without intermission from 7.30 A.M. till late at night. For tutors appointed after that date the number of pupils was limited to forty.

Dr. Warre immediately began to reorganise all this work and to relieve tutors of a considerable part of their burden. Middle and Lower Division—C and D, as they now began to be called, though traces of this method of distinguishing different blocks are found much earlier—did the same Greek lessons and construed these in pupil-room together. It thus became possible to hear all Fifth Form construes in the six periods of half an hour between the end of 9.45 school—which now took place daily instead of only on half-holidays—and the meeting of all masters in Chambers at eleven. Most of the Greek composition was also left to the division master. The whole of C did one copy of verses and the whole of D another, and a school of an hour and a half was set apart for these on Tuesday mornings, so that these blocks cleared off the task, as a rule, by that night. Further steps in the same direction have been taken since

Dr. Warre's time, and to-day only Remove and Fourth Form—E and F—say their lessons to their tutors before going into school. A large number of boys do no Greek and a still larger number substitute a simple piece of Latin prose for verses.

The supervision of a boy's work by his tutor having been so greatly reduced, it might be argued that this dual system had no further excuse for its existence. This, however, is far from being the case. The present system provides an exceptional amount of individual supervision for small boys when they first enter the school. Their Latin exercises are looked over by the tutor, one by one, with the boy standing by his side. Their construing lessons are learnt under his eye and heard in groups of from six to twelve boys, who have an incentive to attention and the use of their memories in the knowledge that they are to be tested in the same piece of work a day or two later. By this constant intercourse a degree of familiarity grows up between tutor and pupil which goes far to mitigate whatever disadvantages there may be in a very large school and which is impossible, except in very rare cases, under the conditions existing between master and boy in the more formal atmosphere of a classroom. Above all it is comparatively easy for a grown-up man to establish really friendly relations with a little boy of from twelve to fifteen years of age, whereas a year or two later the same boy is passing through the shyest and most self-conscious stage of his boyhood, when it is far harder to gain any part of his confidence. The tutorial system ensures that, as far as possible, he shall during that period be in the hands of a man whom he has known for two or three years, and who has had time to size up his capacity, his special difficulties and general point of view.

When boarding houses, with but one or two exceptions, were in the hands of either classical masters or ladies, and the former could be tutor to as many of the boys in his house as he chose, the question of the relations between the housemaster and the tutor hardly arose. But as soon as mathematical and French masters began to hold houses, difficulties were bound to ensue. With respect to his pupil the tutor of a Colleger or of a boy in a dame's house naturally occupied much the same position as that of a housemaster with respect to the boys in his house. He felt himself in charge of the boy both intellectually and morally, and was the regular medium of information about the boy to the parents. To a non-classical housemaster this naturally appeared intolerable. Without his knowledge some young tutor could and did correspond with the father or mother about matters of first-rate importance. As time went on jealousy on one side and want of tact and consideration on the other inflamed a difficult situation, and on several occasions during the last quarter of the nineteenth century friction between the tutor and the housemaster threatened to make this division of control unworkable. Never, probably, was the tutorial system in greater danger ; but wiser counsels fortunately prevailed. It was recognised that the house must be in theory, as indeed it always had been in fact, the centre of a boy's life at school ; that all criticisms, complaints and reports about a boy's conduct and work must be made to the house-master, and that in case of disagreement he must have the final decision in his hands ; and the last thirty years have proved that the difficulty of getting two reasonable men to work together in amicable co-operation is largely imaginary.

One factor which did much to bring about this result was the gradual disappearance of the rigidly classical character of the curriculum. The introduction of a far larger number of subjects necessitated the trans-ference of a good many boys from a classical to a non-classical master's pupil-room ; and a proposal, of which more is said elsewhere,[1] emanating from the joint authors of this book, for the introduction of a scheme which would, incidentally, give all masters a much larger share in the tutorial work of the school, and relieve those who at present bear the bulk of the burden, was not without its effect in showing the protagonists among those who were fighting for the rights of housemasters that some at any rate of the junior classical masters were as anxious as they themselves could be to place all the staff in a position of complete equality and had no desire to maintain the superiority of the classics.

The abolition of the tutorial system has been discussed for more than seventy years. It was criticised by some of the witnesses before the Public

[1] See Chapter IV, pp. 77–8.

Schools Commission, and it was more violently attacked in various magazine articles a few years later. Happily for Eton the critics were confounded and it was realised that this system properly administered is of incalculable value to all concerned. The arguments that have led to this result may be summed up in the words of one, himself educated elsewhere, who later rose to Cabinet rank, when writing a series of articles some thirty years ago on the larger public schools of England.

'You seem', he said, speaking to one of the authors of this book, 'to have devised at Eton a system which, whether it has grown up by design, or accidentally, like the British constitution, produces an almost perfect balance between individual and class teaching. If I had had some one when I was at school to whom I could go, as all these boys seem to come to you, when I was in any difficulty, it would have made simply all the difference to me.'

Not only would the abolition of this system be disastrous to the whole fabric of Eton education, but it is much to be hoped that the solution of one of the most important problems of the moment will lead to its consolidation and extension. At the risk of repetition it must be said once again that this problem arises from the vast increase in the number of subjects which have an undeniable claim to recognition in the curriculum of any school. The present situation is chaotic and boys of quite moderate intelligence flit from subject to subject with a rapidity which precludes real progress in any direction. The whole question has already been discussed in Chapter V ; but it may be said here in conclusion that under present conditions the most gifted boys receive an admirable education, but that the vast majority whose capacity is not above the average are spending their school life without getting more than a confused and superficial knowledge of any subject and therefore without acquiring a real interest in anything intellectual.

CHAPTER IX

THE BLOCK SYSTEM

Trials and Certificates

Although the regulations do not prevent Oppidans from coming to Eton when they are eleven years old, of recent years practically no admission has been made before the age of twelve. As boys may not return to the school after passing their nineteenth birthday, the maximum school life thus lasts seven years. But this figure is very rarely attained. Owing to bad health, change of circumstances, failure to pass examinations or various other causes, about 22 per cent. of those admitted fall early by the way. Excluding these, the normal school course may be said to last just five years ; including them, the average school life of all works out at approximately four years and one Half. The mean age on admission to the school is about thirteen years and three months.

With the exception of Third Form, in which boys usually remain during one schooltime only, it takes, at the ordinary rate of promotion, a year to pass through each block from F to B, though in case of exceptional proficiency double or even treble removes may be granted. The time spent in rising to the top of A necessarily depends on the vacancies caused by boys leaving. School order is unchanged after the school certificate has been obtained.

For purposes of teaching and promotion the school is divided into forms, blocks and removes thus :

Form.		Block.		Number of Boys during the past ten years.		
				Max.	Min.	Average.
Third		F	1 remove only			
Fourth	Lower Boys	F	3rd remove			
			2nd remove	185	104	147
			1st remove			
Remove		E	3rd remove			
			2nd remove	244	190	212
			1st remove			
Fifth, Lower Div.		D	3rd remove			
			2nd remove	241	193	213
			1st remove			
Fifth, Middle Div.		C	3rd remove			
			2nd remove	228	148	192
			1st remove			
Fifth, Upper Div.		B	3rd remove			
			2nd remove	152	43	99
			1st remove			
First Hundred		A	(including Specialists from B)	299	170	239

New boys used to be placed on the results of an examination held at Eton during the first two or three days of each schooltime. Towards the end of Dr. Warre's headmastership this separate examination was replaced by the Common Entrance Examination held at the preparatory schools in the course of the preceding term. This system has obvious advantages for the organisation of the work of lower boys at the beginning of the Half. In former days no lower boy divisions could be made up till the beginning of the second week, whereas now boys return on Wednesday night, all adjustments are made on the Thursday, and with very few exceptions the whole of the school routine is in full swing by 7.30 on Friday morning.

On entry an Oppidan is placed in Third Form, in any of the other three removes of F, or in the third remove of E, a Colleger in the third remove of D. A little before the end of each schooltime all boys, except those competing in external tests, take part in Trials, an examination which lasts six days and covers the work of the current schooltime. On its results depend places and promotion for all who have not got a school certificate. According to the total marks obtained boys are divided into four classes : Distinction, First Class, Second Class and Pass. All these pass into the remove above at the beginning of the next schooltime. Below them come those who fail and lose their promotion. A boy who fails twice running without ample justification is expected to leave the school. There are further difficulties for the idle or incompetent in the shape of superannuation rules which lay down that a boy must be in Fourth Form before reaching his fourteenth birthday, in Remove before reaching his fifteenth, in D by his sixteenth, in C by his seventeenth, and if by his eighteenth birthday he has no prospect of reaching A his further stay at the school is in danger.

The practical working of this promotion system

will perhaps be made clearer by means of concrete instances. X and Y enter the school at thirteen and a quarter, Z comes at thirteen and a half. X is a well-taught boy of decent intelligence who takes Remove, Y is mediocre and takes Middle Fourth, Z is backward and is placed in Third Form. So they start at the beginning of the normal school year in September thus :

X in E, third remove.

Y in F, second remove.

Z in Third Form.

X, unless he falls victim to some serious illness (when his case will be judged on its merits), is sure to have enough in hand to pass in Trials right up the school ; so in September of his second year he will be in the lowest remove of D, of his third year in the lowest remove of C, by his fourth September he will have reached B and will probably take the school certificate without further delay, unless he has already done so. He will then be in A, and free to make a choice of special subjects, at the age of sixteen and a half or seventeen. Y has a longer climb before him. If he does respectably he will be in the middle of E at the beginning of his second year, in the middle of D at the beginning of his third, in the middle of C at the beginning of his fourth ; and, as he will probably need at least a year of school certificate work, he is unlikely to reach A before the age of eighteen, if then.

Z will have a struggle to survive. He is *ex hypothesi* ill-taught or slow or both. If he works hard his first Half he will probably succeed in entering Fourth Form by January, when he is aged 13.10. He is then faced with slightly harder tests as he passes up through F and E and, unless he improves greatly, he will fail to clear either the fifteen-year-old fence from F to E or the sixteen-year-old fence from E to D, and will have to leave.

To make the picture complete one more instance may be given, that of W, a well-taught and intelligent boy just twelve, whose preparatory school is changing hands, so that he wishes to leave early. He comes to Eton in September, not specially prepared and rather flustered, and only takes Upper Fourth. But by the Lent Half of his first school year he has found his feet and shown so much promise that he is given a double remove into D, so that by the beginning of his second year at the age of thirteen he is in the second remove of that block. He will probably end as Captain of the Oppidans.

By long-established tradition, usually though not invariably justified by results, Collegers on entry are placed in the third remove of D. They compete freely with the rest of their remove and move up together with them, though, if reasonably proficient, those who came in January or May are promoted rapidly, so as to catch up those admitted in September. But at the top of the school the first ten places in Sixth Form and the first six immediately below it are reserved for Collegers.

About two hundred and forty-five boys leave annually. Of these approximately half leave in

July, the remainder being distributed almost evenly between December and April. Thus up to about the middle of the school all who pass in Trials will move up roughly a hundred and twenty places in September and sixty in January and May. The occurrence of so many vacancies three times a year renders a corresponding number of promotions inevitable, and these are made through Trials—except that admission to A is obtained through the school certificate examination, held twice yearly in July and December. A rule, for which there is little apparent justification, prohibits most boys from taking this examination before B, though a few from C are allowed to enter for special reasons.

Trials, initiated in their present form by Dr. Warre in 1885, have stood the test of existence practically unchanged for over half a century and deserve some description here. They begin not more than a week before the last day of each schooltime, and during that period boys up to and including B have not less than twelve papers. These mostly last an hour and a half each, and there are three on whole schooldays, two on half-holidays. The papers are intended to cover the whole of the work done in school during the Half. Shortly before the examination begins a booklet is issued containing a time-table, the name of each individual boy with his Trials number, the name of the master in charge of the schoolroom to which he is assigned, the number of the schoolroom and his exact place in it. In each room there are boys from two different blocks, and therefore doing different papers, so that boys doing the same paper do not sit next each other. To facilitate sorting, not more than two blocks are represented in any one room. In order that papers may be more quickly and easily looked over, all those of any length are divided into two parts or even in some cases three. These parts have to be shown up separately, and it is the duty of the master in charge of each room to see that numbers are in their right order and blocks and parts are not confused. When the papers have been worked, he ties each set into a separate bundle, marks the number of his room on it and takes it to the 'Trials Office', a schoolroom set apart for the purpose. Here there are about half a dozen masters who are responsible for checking and distributing papers without delay to those who have to look them over. With each paper are sent two printed sheets containing the name and number of each boy in the block, a column for the entry of the marks obtained and the maximum mark allowed to each part or paper. It should be mentioned here that the Calendar and the Trials booklet give a complete schedule of the marks assigned to each subject in Trials and the standards for 'Distinction', 'First Class', 'Second Class' and 'Pass'. It may also be added that the 'Pass' standard rises in proportion to the time a boy has been in his block. (See pp. 261–68.)

The instant a master has finished looking over a paper—and he is expected to put everything aside in order to attend to it without delay—he sends his completed mark sheet in a printed envelope addressed to the accountant's office. Here on slips already prepared, one for each boy, giving his name and Trials number, the mark is entered in pencil. When complete the slips of each block, sorted into removes, are sent to the master responsible for the block. He, assisted by a suitable number of other masters, adds the marks up, double-checks them, arranges them in order of merit within their removes and enters each name and the mark gained, together with 'Distinctions', 'Classes', 'Passes' and 'Failures', on broad sheets suitable for 'Reading Over' by the Headmaster or Lower Master as the case may be. The slips are then returned to the school office to be sorted ready for distribution to the boys' tutors. The tutors collect and inspect the slips, and send them for transmission home to the house tutor, who has already received their own reports on the boy and those of all other masters who have been teaching him during the schooltime. The division reports are extremely full, dealing not only with a boy's work, but with any noticeable point in his character, and great trouble is taken over their composition. The classical or modern tutor writes a personal letter, often three or four sides of notepaper, to the house tutor—unless the two are identical—giving further details about the boy from a rather different angle. The house tutor, with all the necessary information before him, is then in a position to write his own letter to the parents, summing up and commenting on what others have said, and adding his own reflections about their son's general development.

Nothing has hitherto been said about the setting of the papers, a matter of growing intricacy due to the multiplication of subjects. So far as is possible they are both set and looked over by masters who have not taken part in teaching the individuals concerned. In each block there is a so-called 'block-head' who assigns the setting of papers on divinity, Latin, Greek, and history and geography among a small board formed for the purpose ; mathematics, modern languages and science are arranged by the heads of the departments concerned. For the character and accuracy of the papers set and for dealing with any errors that may occur during their working the heads of blocks and departments are responsible ; the actual administration of the examination while in progress is entrusted to the masters in the Trials office.

After Trials had been in existence for some years an addition was made. For the better boys in B, C and D who aimed at 'Distinction' it was evident that the ordinary school work was insufficient, and the experiment of 'Extra Books' was tried. At first these books consisted merely of a book of Homer or Virgil, read independently out of school and tested before the regular Trials took place. The experiment was successful and ultimately all other main subjects —mathematics, modern languages and the rest— were included, and voluntary reading of a chosen subject became a permanent feature. Finally an English book was included, with the result that now nearly all boys enter for this voluntary examination.

If an internal examination held thrice yearly is to be effective without becoming an incubus, certain objectives must be steadily pursued. In the first place teachers must, as far as practicable, be kept clear of those whom they have taught, so that an unbiassed verdict may be obtained. Secondly, the ordinary hours of school routine must, as far as possible, be retained during the progress of the examination. Thirdly, the examination must be compressed within the narrowest possible compass, so as not to shorten unduly the period of teaching. And lastly, not more than a day should elapse between the end of the examination and the beginning of the holidays. With suitable organisation and the immediate prospect of the holidays a surprising amount of work can be got through within a week, and the delays which occur over the publication of results at some Universities are very hard to understand.

Although Trials in their present form date, as already mentioned, from 1885, both name and idea are older. It should not be forgotten that scholars of King's on the old Foundation—in other words, all Eton masters up to about the middle of the nineteenth century—could proceed to their degrees without examination of any kind, having previously obtained their scholarships by nomination. Examinations seem to have begun for the *élite* as tests for certain definite prizes and distinctions, but for the rank and file to have drifted into existence rather slowly. At any rate, until somewhere between 1870 and 1880, Trials, already a venerable name, were but a hole-and-corner affair, confined to the first remove in each block, that is to those due for promotion, and carried out early in each schooltime in partial interruption of the ordinary routine. When papers were looked over is a mystery, but results were produced somehow late in the Half, and promotions made at once, so that a lower boy on June 4 might be in Fifth Form in July. He could then look forward to a year without examination except for the meaningless Collections (p. 70). Trials of this kind were but a shadow of the present imposing system, but their existence suffices to show that Eton institutions, however modern they may seem, have roots in a dim and perhaps distant past.

Besides Trials there are various external examinations for which some provision has to be made in the curriculum. The chief of these is the school leaving certificate, which is taken by practically all boys. In a normal year there are about 250 boys in the school who have obtained their certificate, and these may devote themselves to any of the groups of subjects mentioned in Chapter IV, p. 75. Of these boys, if they are not to be compelled to leave school early and go to a crammer, some have to be prepared for scholarships in classics, languages, history, mathematics or science ; some for the Navy, Army and Air Force examinations ; others, though they have got a certificate, may have failed to obtain exemption from Responsions or the Previous Examination, and have either to keep up the subject in which they have failed, so as to add it to their certificate, or to take the whole of the University examination. It is therefore necessary to arrange for a dozen or more different courses. That this complicated task is fairly successfully dealt with is proved by the fact that the number of boys who leave the school early because of their inability to pass some examination is negligible.

As the school leaving certificate has been mentioned, a few words may here be said as to its general effect on Eton education. Up to the middle of Dr. Lyttelton's headmastership the only general external examination was the higher school certificate. This came but once a year and was not usually taken till towards the close of a boy's school career. It was confined to boys in First Hundred and by no means all of them ever entered for it. Consequently it had no effect whatever on the work of the average boys in the middle of the school. When the school certificate was substituted for it, the position became quite different. Every boy in C and D knew that in the next year or so he had to face a definite test, and that, till he had passed it, there was no hope of reaching the top block of the school. Those destined for the University—over 60 per cent.—were also aware that by clearing this particular fence they would save themselves an infinite amount of trouble in the future, so that even the idler was tempted by his very idleness to make some effort to succeed. As with all examinations its object may be defeated if attention is devoted to it too exclusively ; and this has unfortunately happened in some schools. But where, as at Eton, it is more or less of an incident in the ordinary course of work, its effects are wholly good. An examination in which boys have no set books that they can learn almost by heart, but have to depend entirely on the knowledge they have acquired and their capacity for displaying it, has a bracing influence.

The higher school certificate, now more generally known as the higher certificate to distinguish it from the school certificate, was introduced at Eton by Dr. Hornby in 1874. As already mentioned, it was not a very satisfactory examination. Whatever the intention of its originators may have been, in the form in which it was adopted at Eton it allowed very little weight to any subject except Latin and Greek. To the latter 1,260 marks were awarded, whereas mathematics had 500, divinity and history only 200 each ; modern languages and science found no place in it. Occasional boys may have done papers in these two subjects, but their marks were ignored in the published list. Another objection was that the examination was spread out over too long a period, as, owing to the requirements of other schools, the papers taken at Eton could not all be set consecutively. Thirdly, the results depended much too largely on the knowledge of set books. The number and length of these were such as to necessitate a two years' course, and it was undesirable to devote so large a portion of the teaching to an examination which many of the boys never intended to take. For a few years the higher certificate and the school certificate existed side by side. Then, in

1912, after a quarter of a century's experience, the former was abandoned.

For many years before either certificate examination was thought of, there had been an annual examination of the first three or four divisions by external examiners. When the higher certificate was introduced those in First Hundred who did not try for a certificate still had to go in for what was known as the First Hundred examination, but the papers were set and looked over by masters. When the higher certificate was abandoned, this First Hundred examination was reorganised under the title of the 'Examination of First Hundred and Specialists'. This is arranged so as to give weight to the various branches of study, and a modern linguist, mathematician, scientist or historian is as likely to head the list as a classical scholar. Numerous scholarships and prizes are awarded on the results of the examination, and the examiners are appointed by the Oxford and Cambridge Joint Board.

CHAPTER X

THE CHAPELS

Their Services and Decoration

Just before the period with which this volume deals considerable changes had been made in the interior of Chapel. The previous history of the treatment of the walls is given fully by Dr. James in his monograph on the Wall Paintings in Eton College Chapel (1929). He shows that the original paintings were executed between 1479 and 1487. Between the latter date and 1560 there had been a little comparatively unimportant mutilation of a few details and a change in the painted framing of the pictures. In 1560 all the paintings were whitewashed over as part of the general crusade against popish ornaments, as is proved by the following entry in the College accounts of that year : 'Item To the Barber for wypinge oute the imagery works vppon the walles in the churche vjˢ viijᵈ'.

This did little harm. But in 1613–14 an organ was erected, probably on the north side, and here the painting has been completely scraped off. Except for the insertion of some painted framework in the classical style, of which a few pilasters can still be traced, no further change took place till 1700, when an organ loft was put up across the building in the second bay from the west, both the north and south walls at this point being painted over. The rest of Chapel, including the westernmost bay, which thus became part of the ante-chapel, was wainscoted to six or eight feet below the window-sills. In 1847 this panelling was replaced by carved oak stalls and canopies in the florid Gothic style then fashionable. The old organ and organ loft were removed and a new organ was put up on the south wall opposite the north door.

At about the same time the windows in the main body of the Chapel were filled with stained glass. The money for the East window was subscribed by, or, as most of them came to think, extorted from, boys in the school during a period of about five years. The side windows, with two exceptions, were given by the Rev. J. Wilder, then a Fellow of the College. A full account of these and of the windows in the ante-chapel [1] may be found in Mr. R. A. Austen-Leigh's *Illustrated Guide to the Buildings of Eton College*. The small window in the west wall above the organ contains far the best glass in the Chapel, made up of all sorts of fragments, most ingeniously arranged to produce a pleasing colour scheme in a symmetrical pattern. This glass appears to date from the fifteenth century and was, perhaps, originally in the other windows in Chapel. Its arrangement and erection in its present position are due to the enterprise and generosity of the Rev.

[1] Those in the ante-chapel in the earlier editions only.

Edward Coleridge, who was an assistant master up to 1850 and subsequently became a Fellow of the College.

During the removal of the panelling it was discovered that the walls on both sides of the western portion of Chapel still had on them the paintings already mentioned, the existence of which had been forgotten. So little importance was, however, attached to them that the clerk of the works took it for granted that they were to be obliterated, and the upper row had been already effaced when Mr. Wilder came in and stopped the destruction of the rest. Despite an appeal from the Prince Consort for some arrangement to be made which might make it possible for the pictures to be seen by those who wished, Provost Hodgson insisted on their being covered up by the Gothic canopies ; and they were not seen again till these were removed at the instance of the Provost, Dr. M. R. James, in 1923. Up to then the only knowledge of them depended on the drawings made by Mr. R. H. Essex immediately after the discovery of 1847.

The uncovering of these paintings raised a difficult problem. In the first place nearly the whole of the top row had disappeared, while in the two spaces where the organ loft of 1700 had stood the traces left were so faint as to be almost unrecognisable. Secondly, the colours, obviously bright and cheerful enough when first laid on, had faded to such an extent as to suggest to Dr. Arthur Benson, Master of Magdalene, as Dr. James records, that 'the place looked like a palaeolithic cavern'. It is true that Professor Tristram, in reproducing upon panels affixed to the gaps an almost exact facsimile of the original scenes, has performed little short of a miracle ; and the restoration of part of the eighteenth-century panelling in the unpainted easternmost bays has done something to improve the general effect. But the lack of colour and the long expanse of bare stone above the panels and the paintings combine to produce an impression of chill and gloom not well suited for any place of worship, and least of all for one used by a congregation of schoolboys. A thoroughly satisfactory solution of the difficulty has not yet been found. Possibly something of the kind suggested ninety years ago by the Prince Consort, with sliding panels of wood or tapestry, may prove eventually to be the best way of dealing with the situation.

After the completion of the alterations begun in 1847 no change of importance took place in the arrangement of Chapel except that the stone pulpit which had then been erected was condemned and replaced by the one still used, which for some time had a sounding board over it ; and the organ was removed from the south wall, and a new one was put up between the chapel and the ante-chapel. This was supported on an erection covered with red baize, which remained an eyesore till in 1881 the present stone screen was given as a memorial to the Old Etonians who had been killed in the Zulu, Afghan and Boer wars. When this was completed it became necessary to construct an almost entirely new organ, as a fire at the builders' works had destroyed the bulk of the old one. The instrument then erected was substantially the one now in use. Its casing and decoration were not completed till 1886. Later it was found that much of the sound was dissipated in the ante-chapel, and in 1902 the disposition of the pipes was altered to cure this defect, and at the same time electric motors were installed instead of the gas engine which had in its turn replaced hand blowing.

Before 1847 all the visible ground space of the Chapel was paved, as the eastern half is now, with black and white marble. At that date this was throughout replaced by the plain stone which still remains in the western portion. The level of this new floor—and to judge by the print in Ackerman's *History of Eton College* (1815) of the one for which it was substituted— was unbroken, except for one low step just to the west of the north door, from the organ screen to within some ten or twelve feet of the altar rails. At this point there was a flight of five or six steps. In 1863 these steps were moved to the altar rails, and no other change in level was made until the complete reflooring of the eastern half of Chapel which formed part of the memorial to the Old Etonians who fell in the South African war of 1899 to 1901. This work was entrusted to Mr. T. B. Carter, a member of a well-known Eton family. By a study of the bases of the columns and other indications visible when the flooring was stripped off, he concluded that in the original design it had been intended to rise to the level of the sanctuary in three stages. Whether this design had ever been carried out before is uncertain. The former black and white marble paving was reproduced over the whole area. A new altar of far more dignified proportions and imposing appearance was substituted for the rather inadequate wooden table of 1850. As the Chapel had ceased to be the Parish Church it was possible for the top of the new altar to be made of marble. The tapestry, made after the design of Burne-Jones by Messrs. Morris at Merton Abbey and presented to the Chapel in 1895 by Mr. Luxmoore, was retained as a reredos and was extended by the addition of two panels so as to cover the whole available width. No one who remembers the previous decoration of the wall behind the altar will regret the alteration.

Two years after his gift of the tapestry, Mr. Luxmoore was instrumental in securing the replica of Watts's Sir Galahad which now hangs on the south wall. Some of his friends urged him to ask the artist, with whom he had a certain amount of acquaintance, if he would paint such a replica and what it would cost. Very unwillingly Mr. Luxmoore consented to do so, though not without some apprehension that he might be giving offence. His apprehension became a certainty when day succeeded day and week week without any acknowledgment of his request. Some months later there arrived for him a large case containing the picture, with a charming letter from Mr. Watts apologising for his silence and explaining that he had been so greatly flattered by Mr. Luxmoore's suggestion that he felt he could not accept any remuneration for what had been a very real pleasure to himself. Would Mr. Luxmoore, therefore, forgive his rudeness and accept the picture as a gift to the Chapel?

To complete the account of what Chapel owes to Mr. Luxmoore, it may here be added that on his retirement from his house in 1902 his old boys, knowing that nothing else would be so acceptable to him, gave him the Cross and Candlesticks that now stand upon the altar.

Of the two side chapels, Lupton's contains the names of those who fell in the South African war; the other, which, unlike Lupton's, is now believed to be part of the original building, has been completely transformed in memory of those killed in the Great War. For a more detailed account of these and other points of interest in Chapel the reader may be referred to the *Illustrated Guide to the Buildings of Eton College* by Mr. R. A. Austen-Leigh.

Something must now be said of the services. One of the most curious facts in connection with Eton in the earlier half of the nineteenth century is the neglect shown by College at that time of the spirit of the statutes and the obvious intention of the Founder. The only weekday services attended by the boys were on whole and half holidays at three o'clock in the afternoon. These services, says Sir Wasey Sterry in his *Annals of Eton College*,

'were gabbled through in the most perfunctory manner, the singing was furnished by the choir of St. George's, Windsor, and that only on Sunday and holiday afternoons, otherwise there was none. The hour of service at Eton prevented the Windsor choir staying beyond the anthem, and thereon followed the somewhat unseemly procedure of the whole choir filing out to reach St. George's in time for the service there.'

He then relates how Henry Dupuis, alluding to this at a Founder's Day dinner, said : 'Mr. Provost, this state of things is intolerable. I, for one, protest against our having only a moiety of Mudge.' Mudge was the St. George's tenor. In these services the boys took no part. Sir Wasey Sterry quotes Mr. Arthur Coleridge as saying : 'We were a cold, stagnant, mute congregation.'

The statement that there was no choir except on Sunday and holiday afternoons requires qualification in one minor point. On Sunday mornings, at any rate for some years before 1864, boys from the Porny School acted in this capacity. That they were a poor substitute for a proper choir is evident from what is said in an article by Mr. A. H. Hall in *The Eton College Chronicle*, of which he was then editor (Nov. 26, 1863).

'The singing on Sunday morning in Chapel', he writes, 'is certainly very bad ; but there is no reason why it should be so. . . . Mr. Snow's [1] kind efforts last Half made a very great improvement for some weeks in the singing at the service which we are writing of, and we believe it was in a

[1] A well-known master at the time who afterwards became Canon Herbert Kynaston.

great measure owing to the "Porny-Boys" not being allowed to sing : certain it is, that their singing (or rather their attempt to do so) deters numbers from joining in. . . . We must add, that we think the College ought not to rely on the congregation for the singing, but provide a proper choir : and we exhort our schoolfellows to do for themselves what they cannot get done for them.'

The agitation of which this article is a symptom proved successful, probably beyond the writer's expectation. In the very next issue (Dec. 10) he is

'happy to be able to state that . . . the Rev. E. Coleridge in his capacity as Precentor, . . . having dispensed with the further services of the "Porny Boys" . . . introduced on Advent Sunday a very tolerable choir, consisting of some of the Teachers and Boys from St. Mark's schools in Windsor.'

In January 1868 matters moved still further. Dr. Hayne, an Old Etonian who had previously been Organist of Queen's College, Oxford, was appointed Precentor (or rather Succentor, as, strictly speaking, a Precentor must be in Orders) and Dr. Elvey and the choir of St. George's disappeared from the scene.

How long Mr. Coleridge's choir from St. Mark's school lasted does not appear to be stated ; but Dr. Hayne on his arrival set to work to collect a proper choir. Meanwhile an effort was made to reinforce the existing choir by seating members of the Musical Society together in Chapel and giving them two or three practices a week.[1] How far this succeeded does

---

[1] *E.C.C.*, Nos. 94 and 109.

not appear, but the tone of the leading article on the subject in the *Chronicle* (109) suggests that the members of the Musical Society had not responded very readily. In any case this expedient was of a very temporary nature. In the second number of the *Chronicle* for the following year we read that 'a New Choir has been organized for the Chapel' and that it 'contains some of the finest voices that can be heard in any church, and has totally dispelled any desire, on the part of the school, to get back the old Choir from St. George's'. It may be of interest to note that Dr. Hayne's name still appears at the head of the stairs leading to New Schools, No. 2 (originally the Music-room) above the letter-box in the small door that gives access to the top of the tower.

From this time onwards the singing in Chapel has steadily improved under the guidance of Dr. Maclean, Sir Joseph Barnby, Dr. Lloyd, Dr. Johnson and Dr. Ley, and the number of visitors who apply for tickets for the Sunday evening services testifies to the excellence of the standard maintained.

In another respect the improvement has been not less marked. Strange though it may appear, up to the time of the Public Schools Commission which issued its report in 1864, no one except the Fellows of the College, and occasionally the Headmaster by their request, was allowed to preach. This is the more curious since at that time two-thirds of the masters were in Orders. Some of the evidence given before the Commissioners on this point is interesting.

Mr. F. E. Durnford, Mr. William Johnson, Mr. Kegan Paul, who were assistant masters at the time, and Viscount Boringdon, an undergraduate who had left Eton a year or two earlier, were questioned as to the advisability of admitting those who were not Fellows to the College pulpit. The first-named was strongly opposed to such a change, chiefly on the ground that boys might in this way hear doctrines which were not strictly orthodox. Mr. Johnson, however, pointed out the absurdity of forbidding men to preach while masters, and then, when they became Fellows at the age of about fifty and had ceased to have any direct contact with the boys, to concede them this right, though he pointed out the possible danger of boys not liking to be preached at by those who exercised direct authority over them in school. Mr. Kegan Paul also approved of the idea and commented on the extreme attention with which boys listened to a preacher if they could hear him. Viscount Boringdon's view of the interest taken in sermons by the boys was not so favourable. When asked whether he thought that sermons could have much beneficial effect on boys he replied : 'I do not think I often heard a sermon that would'! and added that the sermons preached by the Fellows were not easily heard by the boys 'and if they were I do not think they would be much attended to'.

Before this same Commission the suggestion was also made that preachers from outside Eton should be occasionally introduced. To those of the present generation who have heard Dr. Alington's sermons and bedtime stories, to say nothing of other distinguished preachers, the notion that the pulpit should be the monopoly of a very limited number of old men, worn out by years of overwork as masters, can appear nothing but preposterous. But seventy years ago it required all the energy and authority of a very exceptional Royal Commission to disabuse men's minds of this ridiculous prepossession.

The contrast between the idea that no Eton master was fit to preach in Chapel, and the establishment under Dr. Warre of the principle that the preparation of boys for Confirmation was among a housemaster's most important duties, is only one rather extreme instance of the many silent revolutions that have been taking place at Eton during the last seventy years. Now that housemasters are almost exclusively laymen this preparation is supplemented by addresses given to Confirmation candidates by some member of the clergy specially invited for the purpose.

Up to the time of Dr. Balston's retirement from the headmastership at the end of 1867 the whole of the upper school—all boys, that is, down to the bottom of Fourth Form (see p. 29)—had been crowded into the College Chapel. 'In the days of Dr. Goodford and Dr. Balston, the Lower School, that is to say all the boys below the Fourth Form, attended divine service on week days in the Cemetery Chapel on the Eton Wick Road, and on Sundays in St. John's Chapel in the High Street of Eton' (Maxwell Lyte). In the first half of Dr. Goodford's headmastership, while the upper school varied in number between 550 and 600 boys, the accommodation was at any rate sufficient. But by the end of Dr. Balston's time the figure had risen to over 750 and the crowding had become intolerable. One of Dr. Hornby's first measures was to institute services for Fourth Form (180 boys) in the music-room of New Schools—a room in the tower on the Slough Road which has now been transformed into two schoolrooms (Nos. 14 and 15). In *The Eton College Chronicle* of the time (No. 107) this was hailed as a great improvement, though how 180 boys, even small boys, were compressed into the space that now accommodates two divisions of between thirty and forty apiece will puzzle anyone who knows the rooms. Previously the congregation of College Chapel had overflowed into Lupton's Chapel, and, even so, many fainted during the hot weather in the summer of 1865. Later a temporary building was erected at the bottom of Keate's Lane, close to South Meadow. In 1875, before this was built, the editors of the *E.C.C.* asserted that the extension of New Schools completed two years later would 'contain a spacious chapel for the Fourth Form'. Whether this was ever really contemplated is uncertain, but in any case lower boys were subsequently accommodated in the building just described.

Eventually, after the Queen's Schools had been completed in 1889, the present Lower Chapel was put in hand. It was completed in 1891, and the dedication service formed part of the proceedings on the occasion of the celebration of the four hundred and fiftieth anniversary of the College. A full account of this chapel is given by Mr. Austen-Leigh in his *Guide to the Buildings of Eton College*. Up to 1920 the bare stone walls produced a rather cold effect; but since then the interior has been completely transformed as part of the Memorial to the Old Etonians who fell in the Great War. The first step in this process was the extension along the whole of the south wall of the aisle, of which two bays had been added to the original building some years after its completion, to provide accommodation for visitors. This extension was finished in 1923. Of the decoration of the interior the *E.C.C.* of November 15, 1923, gives the following account :

'The War Memorial in Lower Chapel comprises the panelling of the north and south walls in a renaissance design of darkened oak, ebony and gold, tapestries on the north wall, and the treatment of the organ case and pews to bring them in harmony with the new work. The scheme of woodwork on the walls is carried over the canopies of the return stalls ; and a little west of the sanctuary it is terminated by pillars on which are painted the arms of Winchester, Oxford and New College on the north side, and of King's, Cambridge and the Bishopric of Lincoln on the south. In the spandrels of the southern arcade the arms, emblematic of the principal regions of the war, are (from the eastern end) those of the Christian Kings of Jerusalem, the Emperors of Constantinople, the Cinque Ports, the Counties of Artois and Flanders, Verona, Ypres, and St. Omer. Commemorative inscriptions to the east of the stalls are surmounted by the coats of Eton College and the Founder.'

The tapestries alluded to above, which were not completed till later, now form the chief glory of the Chapel. They were produced at the Merton Abbey Works from the designs of Lady Chilston—then Mrs. Akers Douglas. There are four panels representing scenes from the life of St. George, the patron saint of England and of soldiers. The first panel from the west suggests the education of a boy, idealised in the character of St. George. The background is reminiscent of Windsor Castle and some of the Eton buildings. The arms of Provosts Waynflete, Lupton, Wotton and Godolphin are shown in the four corners.

The second panel is an allegory of Belgium's appeal to England for help against Germany, the struggle with the dragon being symbolical of Germany's defeat. The arms in the four corners are those of four distinguished Etonian generals— Plumer, Rawlinson, Byng and Cavan.

In the third panel are shown St. George's refusal to serve the Emperor Diocletian, the persecutor of the Christians, his martyrdom and his reception in Heaven, where he is seen kneeling on the sea of glass and fire (Rev. xv. 2). In the corners are the arms of four deceased Etonian generals—Roberts, Maude, Thesiger and Fitton.

The last panel suggests that the participation of Great Britain in the war was of the nature of a crusade, and episodes of St. George's life in this connection are consequently depicted. He appears in the sky to save from shipwreck the vessel that was carrying Richard Cœur de Lion to the Holy Land, and, with St. Demetrius, comes to the help of the crusaders in the battle of Antioch (1098). In the centre he stands on the cliffs of England to bless our forces. The arms are those of Dr. James, Mr. H. V. Macnaghten, Dr. Alington and Mr. A. B. Ramsay, respectively Provost, Vice-Provost, Headmaster and Lower Master in 1923.

The Chapel, as now arranged, will seat about five hundred and fifty people. Of these seats the boys occupy about four hundred and seventy. Two of the bays of the aisle, capable of holding about seventy in all, are reserved for masters and their families, dames and visitors, while stalls and desks accommodate another twelve or fifteen masters. In College Chapel the former crowding has been much relieved by the enlargement of Lower Chapel, and, excluding about eighty seats for masters and visitors, it now provides places for about six hundred and sixty boys. These figures vary slightly from Half to Half according to the number of Roman Catholics and members of other denominations in the school. A comparison of the figures given for the two buildings will show how large a part Lower Chapel now plays. It should also be mentioned that the boys provide the whole of its choir. The result, both as regards the music and the general tone of the services, is highly satisfactory.

Although in the last sixty years many important changes have been made in the times and arrangement of services in Chapel, the Headmaster cannot demand, but can only tentatively suggest, that any change should be made. The appointment of the Precentor, the maintenance of the choir and the choir school, the hours, length and character of the services, and the choice of preachers are all matters which come under the sole jurisdiction of the Provost. Possibly the Bishop of Lincoln, as Visitor, might in wholly exceptional circumstances have some claim to exercise an overriding authority, but even this is highly problematical. This curious anomaly has in recent years been extended to include Lower Chapel.

The origin of this state of affairs lies in the history of the foundation of Eton. The College is a Royal Foundation and the Provost is appointed by the Crown. In old days the death or retirement of a Provost was considered to entail almost automatically the selection of the existing Headmaster to succeed him. Lord Palmerston, for instance, on the death of Dr. Hawtrey recommended Dr. Goodford as his successor without even waiting to ascertain if the latter wished for the change. This being so, it was perhaps not unnatural that the Provostship should carry with it the control of the Chapel. Up to the present no real difficulty has been caused by the existence of these two authorities side by side. But it is obvious that circumstances might arise which would cause friction. What the ultimate solution may be no one can foretell. At the moment the identity of interests between the Provost and Fellows on the one hand and the school, as represented by the Headmaster, on the other is being more and more clearly recognised and their co-operation is becoming increasingly cordial.

CHAPTER XI

BIRTH OF A NEW ETON

An architectural tour

If someone who was at Eton in 1860 could be re-
suscitated and put down on Barnes Pool Bridge, the
first thing he would notice, besides the alterations in
the High Street behind him—the growth of buildings
and the absence of fields—would be the replacement
of the comparatively narrow bridge of his day by the
present flat and featureless structure, which, though
described by J. K. Stephen as a 'never-sufficiently-
to-be-damned piece of ugliness', was fortunately so
strongly built in 1884 that it successfully carries the
enormously increased weight of modern traffic. On
leaving the bridge he would be struck by the change
from a heterogeneous collection of little shops to the
attractive frontage presented since 1932 by the School
Stores. As he proceeded along the left-hand side of
the road he would find little change in the exterior
of Gulliver's, Jourdelay's, the Christopher, Hodgson
House, the Bookshop, or Carter House, except that
between the two last named 'Little Brown's' had
ceased to exist as a sock shop. But, if he turned in
through the archway between the Christopher and
Hodgson House, he would find that Charlie Wise's
stables had vanished, and that their place had been

taken by additions to a much-enlarged Hodgson House, while 'Pop' rooms had been transferred to the opposite side of the yard.

Crossing the top of Keate's Lane he would still find familiar landmarks in Hawtrey House and Durnford House ; but would be startled to see, in place of the little low building known to him as Drury's and the tall, gaunt yellow-brick monstrosity inhabited and added to by Wolley-Dod, the imposing, if over-ornamented façade of the School Hall and Library. Enquiry would reveal to him that these were a memorial to Old Etonians who fell in the South African war and that the former was completed in 1908, the latter in 1910. Entering the building he would also be shown the room adapted for the Millington Drake collection of books on the Great War, and the new museum designed by Mr. Edmond Warre to house the Myers Egyptian collection originally placed in that room.

Leaving the School Hall, our wayfarer will notice, perhaps not without regret, that though, except for the reconstruction of the private part in 1863, the fabric of the Manor House is unchanged, it has been stripped of the plaster the mellow tones of which were a feature of that part of Eton. Passing on down Common Lane he will find very little change on the left-hand side of the road, though he may wonder at the size of Common Lane House and Penn House. Nothing else will excite his attention unless on reaching the white gate he penetrates into the kitchen garden of Warre House, in which case he

will see, where he expected pigstyes, an unknown
residence overlooking the waters of Babylon. Here
his attention will be attracted by the pumping station
connected with the sewage farm—a successful piece
of architecture which, thanks to the skill of its
designer, Mr. T. B. Carter, is a far from unpleasing
object ; by the brick arches of the G.W.R. viaduct
which in 1861 replaced the wooden piles of his boyhood ; and beyond these by the chimneys of the Sanatorium that he knew, now, however, surrounded by
the roofs of the little hamlet which has sprung up to
meet the demand for additional cottage accommodation after the war.

When he returns to Common Lane he will be
startled. The road that now runs at the level of the
street over a bridge to the pumping station was in
his day a track across a low-lying meadow with a ford
through the stream, spanned by a single rickety
plank. Between Common Lane and Jordan he
would expect no buildings of any sort except the gasworks which occupied the site of the present parade
ground ; the house now known as Angelo's ; a
small group of buildings (replaced in 1905 by the
Warre Schools) comprising a pupil-room, a cottage
and the School of Arms—this last being a combination
of a fencing and boxing school with a rudimentary
gymnasium, managed for four generations by the
Angelos, one of whom occupied the house known by
their name ; and the Hopgarden, now completely
transformed. With these exceptions there was in his
time nothing between Common Lane and Jordan but

a paddock and some gardens with the School Field beyond. It was not till some of the Fives Courts were erected in 1870 that this ground began to be used for building. In 1879 Dr. Warre had the Drill Hall and School of Mechanics put on the site which they occupied until 1926, when their place was taken by the large block of schoolrooms and greatly improved workshop known as the Drill Hall Schools. Then, having been made Headmaster and finding himself cramped for room in Savile House, which at that time included the northern portion at present used as a masters' colony, he built Colenorton. After this there was a pause till the appointment of Mr. Hollway-Calthrop as Bursar in 1900 inaugurated a spell of activity. In 1904 accommodation was provided for the manager of Messrs. Spottiswoode's bookshop and a printing press (called the Savile Press); and four years later this building was completed by the addition of the Caxton rooms with a storeroom for the workshop below them. In 1907 a gymnasium was built at the instance of Dr. Lyttelton, and in 1910 a miniature range was installed in the upper portion of it. Thus all the available space in this part of Eton was filled.

At the back of these buildings our old-time visitor will find a new world. Turning out of Common Lane between the Drill Hall Schools and the Caxton Schools he will emerge on to an asphalt parade ground where he recollected the squalor and smell of the gasworks. In front of him he will see the Drawing Schools and Picture Gallery, the main portion of which was a memorial to Captain Geoffrey Prideaux, who was killed in 1917. It was finished in 1923. The forecourt was added a year or two later in memory of another Old Etonian, Major Evan Hanbury, killed in 1918.

As he approaches this building he will notice a charming little sunken garden commemorating Prince Frederick Victor Duleep Singh, who was at Eton from 1881 to 1883. On the right his attention will be attracted by a lofty and dignified wall forming the back of the new range of covered Fives Courts and broken by an archway, on one side of which stands the Fives Courts branch of the School Stores. Such covered courts are a comparatively new institution at Eton. The two first built are those at the northern end of the range. They were put up in 1906 by Mr. Marten, treasurer of the Fives fund, and Mr. Churchill, who had recently succeeded to a house. Of the remaining thirteen, six were built through the generosity of Sir John Mullens and Mr. E. L. Gosling, while the cost of the seven others and of the School Stores building was defrayed by Mr. W. H. Askew (now Askew-Robertson) as part of his many benefactions. The first eight courts were finished in 1923, the rest of the scheme was not completed till the end of 1925.

The mention of Mr. Askew makes this an appropriate place to enumerate his other gifts to the school. Besides contributing between four and five thousand pounds to the Drawing Schools, he made himself responsible for the whole of the new organ

in the School Hall, as well as the panelling at
the west end designed by Mr. Powell to fit in
with the old Rotterdam organ and case acquired
many years previously by Mr. Luxmoore. This cost
approximately £9,000. The installation of electric
light and a proper heating system in Chapel is also
his work. The school is indebted to him for these
very much needed improvements to the value of
nearly £25,000. If all the Old Etonians who
grumble that more such luxuries are not provided out of funds barely sufficient for necessities
would follow his example according to their means,
all their demands could soon be satisfied. In time
to come Mr. Askew-Robertson's name will doubtless
be included in the list of benefactors from which a
selection is read in Chapel on Founder's Day; but it
is to be hoped that the honour may be long deferred,
as by an immemorial custom no one is admitted to
this dignity till he is dead.

Our nonagenarian, surprised at finding fifty-three
Fives Courts to replace the eight or ten that he
remembers on the Dorney Road (pulled down in
1935 to make room for an additional boys' house),
passes between the open and covered courts to the
Racket Courts and Squash Courts—all equally new
to him, having been built, the former in 1902–3, the
latter at various dates in the last thirty or forty years.
Proceeding across Sixpenny [1] he will find that it has

---

[1] A meadow used in summer for cricket under the name of Sixpenny,
in winter for football under that of the Field, and officially known in
all seasons as the Timbralls.

been further encroached upon by two houses, of which one, built in 1863, takes its name from its site on the Timbralls, the other dates from 1903 and now has attached to it a Squash Court given by the parents of J. H. Caldwell as a memorial to their son, who was killed in the Great War.

He will also notice further away on his left that Fifteen Arch Bridge has been widened and enormously improved in appearance (1936), and that near the one building at Willowbrook which he remembers there have now sprung up about half a dozen other residences besides the extensive range of buildings of the Eton School Laundry, established by a few masters about 1888 as a private company, which has proved a great boon to all boys whose housemasters make use of it. One of the writers well remembers the delight of finding wet football or beagling clothes taken away each evening and returned dry and clean before noon next day, instead of having to face the discomfort of putting them on, clammy and cold, after unsuccessful attempts to deal with them in front of a small fire.

Reaching the corner of Sixpenny by the Slough Road, where, in view of his age, he will no doubt be relieved to discover that he need not clamber over a muddy stile, he will be puzzled by the appearance of the buildings on the other side of the road which have undergone considerable alterations, but these have been so skilfully carried out by Mr. Edmond Warre that the keenest eye can hardly distinguish between old and new. He will be more bewildered when he turns to the right expecting to find a paddock and garden instead of the massive brickwork of New Schools. The two halves of these were built at different times. The earlier block, facing the Manor House, bears the date 1863 ; the later, facing the Slough Road, 1876. He will also observe that the old street lamp that he knew in the centre of the space where the Slough Road and Common Lane converge has been replaced by the ornate erection almost ever since irreverently called 'The Burning Bush'.

As the Birdcage, the Long Wall, Upper School and Chapel are unchanged since he left, except for the addition of the Waynflete Memorial to the west end of the last named, our very Old Etonian turns into Weston's Yard. Passing through, while welcoming the grass plots which have replaced the dreary expanse of dusty gravel, he will no doubt regret the disappearance of the School Library, known as the Hawtrey Library, which formed part of the College New Buildings put up in 1846, and the taste of those responsible for the additions made in 1885. This feeling will, however, be changed to one of delight when he passes through the archway and sees the transformation effected by the removal of the high brick wall which, with the College stables, used to hide the view of the Provost's Lodge from the north. The beauty of the view has been further enhanced by King Prajadhipok's sunken garden in the foreground. The new garages between this and the river are also worthy of notice as an instance of how well a purely utilitarian modern building can be made to harmonise with an ancient setting.

The cloisters will present a few novelties. The transference of the Headmaster's house to this position has been recorded in another chapter. The memorial tablets form a striking contrast to the bareness of the old walls; and the additions required by the threatened collapse of Lupton's Tower afford another example of Mr. Edmond Warre's skilful adaptation of architectural necessity to its surroundings. The removal of a portion of the railings on the west side of the cloister, and the lowering of those on the north and east sides by the demolition of the low wall on which they rested, will also probably strike our visitor as an improvement.

In School Yard he will note at first only two minor alterations—the removal of the railings on either side of Lupton's Tower and the appearance on the north and east sides of two blocks of stone which when first placed there in 1884 roused the indignation of a correspondent in the *Chronicle* who compared them to wine-cases. But at the western end, in the colonnade under Upper School, he will pause for a time to examine the war memorial with its dignified oak ceiling and tragic list of names.

Retracing his steps he will notice in the south-east corner a new entrance to the churchyard—the name with which he will be familiar, as Chapel was in his time still the chief parochial church of Eton and remained so legally till 1875, though St. John's church in the High Street was completed in 1854.

He will also find that the nineteenth-century archway between School Yard and Brewer's Yard has been replaced by a wall and door. Passing through the latter he will see nothing new except the exit to the road running along Baldwin's Shore—a euphemism for Baldwin's Sewer, an open waterway which till 1845 ran along the line of the present road. Above the archway between this and Brewer's Yard stands a passage of which one end is now left in the air. This was added in 1891 to connect the buildings on either side which had for many years formed a single boys' house and continued to do so until the fire of 1903 destroyed the western and larger half. Five years later a small house was built for Mr. Luxmoore on the site, but by a grievous error in alignment, due to the refusal of the tenant of Baldwin's Bec to allow the obstruction of a perfectly unnecessary window, this new house has been set back at an angle that leaves a gap at the end of what had been a passage.

From here our visitor is conducted by his guide through Jourdelay's to the point where the Dorney Road leaves Keate's Lane, his attention being attracted in passing by the towering chimney that forms the apex of the large new portion of Hodgson House built in 1903. When he reaches the junction of the roads, the only building he recognises in front of him or to his left will be Keate House, though on his right Keate's Lane looks much as it did in his time. Where he expects to see the insignificant line of the old Mathematical Schools, with the Rotunda rising in the background, he is confronted with the large block of the Queen's Schools (1889), Lower Chapel (1891), and the Museum, part of which was added in 1904 as a memorial to the two boys who lost their lives in the fire at Baldwin's End. Further down the road the site of what had been at one time Lower Chapel, at another a music-room, is occupied by South Lawn—the private part built in 1869 by Dr. Hayne, the boys' house added in 1905. On the opposite side of the lower half of Keate's Lane are various buildings, which have passed through many phases. They contained during the last quarter of the nineteenth century two Racket Courts, some additional school-rooms and a chemical laboratory, all unknown to him. In 1903 the Racket Courts were transformed into music schools. Since that date additional laboratory accommodation has been provided in the same group of buildings ; later two new school-rooms were erected, and finally in 1936 these last and the chemical laboratory were replaced by a fine block of rooms known as the Montague James Schools.

As our now wellnigh exhausted traveller proceeds along the Dorney Road to Judy's Passage—known to him as Carter's Passage—he will miss the only Fives Courts he ever knew, but the growth in the size of the school shown by the new houses on both sides of him will be a revelation. On his left is Walpole House (1907) ; just beyond it a new boys' house, not complete at the time of writing, which is to occupy the site of the house called Mustians built by Mr. A. C. Ainger on his retirement. Opposite these are Waynflete House (1899), Westbury House (1900), and, on the other side of Judy's Passage, Cotton Hall House (1870). Beyond this the Briary and the adjoining cottages complete the tale.

In Judy's Passage there is little to notice except the boys' part of Holland House rebuilt in 1880, and the new passage opened within the last decade between Warre House and Penn House.

This geographical tour of Eton shows the changes that have taken place in the external appearance of the school; but it leaves obscure certain striking points which require elucidation.

In the first place, in view of recent criticism directed against the College authorities for their failure to keep the houses in the condition nowadays considered desirable, it is of the utmost importance to give some idea of the situation with which they were faced towards the end of the last century. This can be most easily done in tabular form, and the lists following have been compiled for the purpose.

No. 1 shows the houses that existed as boys' houses before the time of the Public Schools Commission;

No. 2 those that were added between 1862 and 1900;

No. 3 those that have been built in the present century.

To No. 1 must be added a few small houses which formerly sometimes accommodated eight or ten boys, and sometimes were used as private residences. These have long ceased to be used as boarding houses.

1	2	3
Before 1862	1862–1900	1900–1936
Angelo's	Cotton Hall House	Wotton House
Baldwin's Bec	(1870)	(1903)
*Baldwin's End	Waynflete (1899)	South Lawn
*Baldwin's Shore	Westbury (1900)	(1905)
Carter House		Walpole House
*Christopher		(1907)
Coleridge House		Mustians
Common Lane House		(1936)
*2 Common Lane		
Corner House		
Durnford House		
Evans'		
Godolphin House		
Gulliver's		
Hawtrey House		
Hodgson House		
Holland House		
Hopgarden		
Jourdelay's		
Keate House		
Manor House		
Penn House		
Timbralls		
Warre House		
*Weston's		*Have ceased
**Two houses formerly		to exist as
on site of School Hall.		boys' houses

The houses in List 1 varied almost infinitely in size and amenities. All but two or three of the best and biggest of these, built at the end of the period, have been enlarged and improved so as to comply with a standard of uniformity previously regarded as unnecessary. Seven of the houses have ceased to exist as boarding houses, and an eighth (Gulliver's) has been converted into a holding house in which fifteen or sixteen boys—half the previous number—are accommodated for a period which may never exceed a year, after which they move on to a full-sized house. In spite of all efforts, however, it has been found impossible to bring half a dozen of the older houses up to the level of the rest, but it is hoped that the new ten-years building-scheme inaugurated with Mustians will cure this defect.

List 2 shows that the second period was one of inactivity on the part of the College authorities. This was even more marked than appears, for Cotton Hall House was built by private enterprise, while Waynflete and Westbury really form part of a series of new houses planned at the extreme end of last century. It is true that the boys' part of Holland House was practically rebuilt in 1880 after the old house had been vacant for three years and the site had nearly been used for an hotel, but this seems to be the only operation of any importance that was undertaken. The causes of this were twofold. Firstly, as appears from the report of the Public Schools Commissioners, the College, though owning

twenty-three of the thirty boarding houses then existing, had lost control of them by granting long leases
which had passed into the hands of tenants wholly
unconnected with the school. Secondly, from 1868
to 1900 the man who, both by his personality and
his office, was the ruling spirit of the Governing Body
was the Bursar, the Rev. W. A. Carter. It is not to
be wondered at that one brought up in the traditions
of the Provost and Fellows of the middle of last
century was slow to agree to new schemes involving
large expenditure.

Consequently, when at the extreme end of the
century the College under the influence of Dr.
Warre became alive to the necessities of the situation, it had to face simultaneously serious arrears of
reconditioning and a large amount of new construc-
tion. Ill-health compelled Mr. Carter's successor to
resign in less than a year and the appointment of
Mr. Hollway-Calthrop to the bursarship introduced
a new epoch.

It must not be imagined that the length of time
that has elapsed between the building of Walpole
House and Mustians means that this energetic policy
has in any way flagged. It is hardly an exaggeration
to say that in this period there is no house, whether
boarding or otherwise, that has not been enlarged or
improved. It must be remembered, too, that during
the Great War and the years immediately succeeding
it such operations had to be reduced to a minimum,
while the industrial troubles that culminated in the
general strike of 1926, followed by the financial

difficulties of 1929 and the subsequent years, made the position scarcely less difficult.

In spite of these obstacles much has been done in other directions, as will appear from the following list, in which the period has been divided into two halves—namely from 1864 to 1900 and from 1901 to 1936. Of the items marked *c* the original cost was borne by College,[1] of those marked *p* by private individuals or subscription.

Though the latter were originally financed by private enterprise it must be remembered that, through the expiry of leases or by purchase or otherwise, they have since then passed to College.

LIST 4

A. 1864–1900

1864–70   *p* Cotton Hall House.
       p Common Lane House, boys' part only.
       p The Briary.
       p Upper Club Pavilion.
       p Eight Fives courts (thirty more added gradually).

[1] For the greater part of the period under review the income of College, derived from land and, to a trifling extent, from endowments, was kept completely separate from the income of the school, derived from school fees. Up to 1920 the school often had some difficulty in making both ends meet, while the College, by borrowing or by the sale of some of its land, could raise money when required. This process, however, has impoverished the College. Latterly the rigid distinction between the two funds has tended to disappear, and in some cases it has been the school fund that has provided the money for new buildings. As the interests of the two bodies are obviously identical the letter *c* is used to include both funds indifferently.

1871–80   *c* Holland House, boys' part rebuilt.
         c New Schools Nos. 16–31, originally Mathematical Schools.
         p Upper Club Pavilion enlarged.

1881–90   *c* College Sickrooms.
         c Briary Cottage.
         c Queen's Schools (nine rooms and Science Museum).
         p Queen's Schools, Lecture Room.
         p Colenorton.
         p Laundry.

1891–
   1900   *c* Waynflete.
         c Westbury.
         c Briary End.
         c Burnham Thorpe reconditioned.
         c Two Queen's Schools Laboratories—one originally a Drawing School.
         cp Lower Chapel.
         p Two Squash courts.
         p Kennels and Kennelman's cottage.

B. 1901–1936

1901–10   *c* Wotton House.
         c Walpole House.
         c South Lawn, boys' part only.
         c Hodgson House, half boys' part.
         c Baldwin's End.
         c Warre Schools (eight rooms).

c Caxton Rooms (two rooms).

c Science Schools (three rooms, four laboratories, Lecture Room).

c One Queen's Schools laboratory.

c Music Schools (eight rooms and organ room).

c Savile Press and Manager's house.

c Gymnasium—Miniature Range added later.

c Two Racket courts.

c Two cottages in Agar's Plough.

cp Pavilion in Agar's Plough.

cp Rebuilding of organ in College Chapel.

cp Boathouses all purchased and part reconstructed.

p Science Museum extension.

p School Hall and Library with Myers Museum.

p Willowbrook Cottage and Stream Corner.

p Cricket Shed for indoor practice.

p Two covered Fives courts.

p Five Squash courts.

1911–20 *p* Willowbrook End.

p The Marches, Willowbrook.

p One Squash court.

p Shelter in Agar's Plough.

1921–30 *c* Drill Hall Schools (ten rooms).

c Mechanical School.

c Fellows Garden garages.

p Drawing Schools (four rooms) and Picture Gallery.

p Organ in School Hall.

p New heating system and electric light in College Chapel.

p Parade Ground.

p Thirteen covered Fives courts.

p School Stores Fives courts branch.

p Four Squash courts.

p Babylon.

p Luxmoore and Prajadhipok gardens.

1931–36   *c* Mustians.

c Keate Schools (ten rooms).

c School Stores—Barnes Pool.

p New Myers Museum and Millington-Drake (or Macnaghten's) Library.

p Cinema in School Hall.

p Duleep Singh garden.

p Eight hard Lawn Tennis courts.

p Two open Fives courts covered.

p Temporary Sheds replaced by new Boathouse.

The following summary will show more clearly the present position of the school as regards equipment, and will bring out the contrast between the comparative inactivity of the authorities in the earlier and their activity in the later period.

SUMMARY OF LIST 4
1864–1900

Lower Chapel.
Boys' houses . . . . . 5 new
College Sickrooms.
Residences . . . . 5 „
Schoolrooms . . . . 25 „
Science Museum.
Lecture room.
Laboratories . . . . 2 „
Fives courts . . . . 38 „
Squash courts . . . . 2 „
Laundry.
Upper Club Cricket Pavilion.
Kennels and Kennelman's cottage.

1901–1936

School Hall and Library.
Myers Museum and Millington-Drake
 Library.
Organ and Cinema in School Hall.
Boys' houses . . 4 new ; 1 rebuilt
Residences . . . . 6 new
Savile Press and Manager's house.
Schoolrooms . . . . 37 „
Mechanical School.
Music rooms . . . . 8 „
Organ room.
Gymnasium and Miniature Range.
Science Museum extension.

Picture Gallery.
Lecture room.
Laboratories . . . . 5 new
College Chapel—heating & lighting.
    ,,   ,, —rebuilding organ.
School Stores—Barnes Pool.
    ,,   ,, —Fives Courts.
Cottages in Agar's Plough . . 2 ,,
Pavilion in Agar's Plough.
Cricket shed.
Shelter in Agar's Plough.
Boathouses.
Racket courts . . . . 2 ,,
Covered Fives courts . . . 15 ,,
Roofing of open Fives courts . 2 ,,
Squash courts . . . . 10 ,,
Hard Lawn Tennis courts . . 8 ,,
Parade Ground.
Gardens . . . . . 3 ,,
Garages.

It appears from list 4 that, small as was the part played by College in providing boarding houses in the earlier of the two periods under discussion, it was even smaller in other respects, especially in the first twenty years.

The following synopsis may serve to make still clearer the situation revealed by these lists.

Since 1860 twelve new Oppidan houses (out of a total of twenty-six) have been built, and all but two of the rest have been materially enlarged and improved.

Besides the buildings devoted exclusively to science and to the subjects classed in Chapter V as extra subjects, seventy-eight schoolrooms (out of a total of eighty-three) are new since 1863.

Much of the comfort now enjoyed by the Collegers is due to additions made in 1885 ; and of their living accommodation before that date only a quarter existed before 1846.

Of the two chapels one is less than fifty years old and the interior of the other was completely transformed between 1843 and 1850, and its appearance has again been very greatly altered in the last thirty-five years.

All the buildings connected with outdoor recreation, together with two-thirds of the football and cricket fields, have been built or acquired since 1864.

The striking fact therefore emerges that, notwithstanding the air of antiquity that pervades the school, practically all its material requirements have been supplied within the lifetime of the oldest of Old Etonians.

CHAPTER XII

UNIFORMITY AND UNIFORM

Costume, Corps and Scouts

Though there has been no fundamental change in the ordinary school dress during the last seventy years, the answers given by Dr. Balston, the Headmaster, in his evidence before the Public Schools Commission are curious.

'One more question', says the Chairman, 'which bears in some degree on other schools, namely with regard to the dress. The boys do not wear any particular dress at Eton?'

To this the Headmaster replied:

'No, with the exception that they are obliged to wear a white neckcloth.' [1]

'Is the colour of their clothes much restricted?'

'We would not let them wear for instance a yellow coat or any other colour very much out of the way.'

'If they do not adopt anything very extravagant either with respect to colour or cut you allow them to follow their own taste with respect to the choice of their clothes?'

'Yes.'

---

[1] At that date either a white stock or a collar and white tie were permissible. By 'turn-down collars' the Headmaster obviously means what are now called Eton collars.

211

Lord Lyttelton then asked :

'They must wear the common round hat ?'

'Yes.'

Lord Devon continued :

'How far down in the school does the wearing of the white neckcloth go ?'

'It does not extend to those who wear turn-down collars.'

'Do many of the boys wear stick ups ?'

'Yes, and they must then wear a white tie.'

According to the Headmaster it appears then that boys might wear whatever costume they liked, short of anything outrageously glaring or absurd, provided it included a white neckcloth or a white tie. The hat was to be 'the common round hat', which presumably meant a top-hat. Beyond this there was no official school dress. Yet tradition, old prints and the memory of men still alive make it clear that long before 1860 all boys wore clothes which did not differ fundamentally from those in use at the present day. It is only necessary to look at photographs of the house groups of that time to see that the black coat and waistcoat with either a turn-down or stick-up collar, or the Eton jacket and Eton collar, were as much *de rigueur* then as now. Yet the Headmaster knew nothing of this as a school rule and would apparently have endured without a murmur the apparition of his Sixth Form in pepper-and-salt lounge suits and brown shoes provided only that their necks were encircled by a white choker or a collar and white tie.

So this dress, which we have all regarded as

established by a law as unalterable as those of the Medes and Persians, turns out to have been merely another of the unwritten regulations made by the boys themselves. Instances of the same kind will occur to anyone who has been in close touch with Eton for the last thirty or forty years. One particularly striking case is connected with the style of cloth used for the everyday school trousers. A house group of 1903 shows thirty or forty boys in a well-known house whose nether garments are made of various tweeds or other kinds of cloth, but not of the striped variety now in fashion. Public taste had, perhaps, toned down the patterns that were popular, but otherwise there had not been much change for thirty or forty years. Then suddenly in 1905 another house group reveals that every boy is wearing striped trousers of the modern type. In this short period fashion has produced a revolution, and a boy who wore any other kind of school suit would be an object of derision. Other earlier groups show that the braid on the edges of the coat and waistcoat, now reserved for members of 'Pop', was then a matter of the boys' own choice. Again, between 1880 and 1890, each big boy decided for himself when he had attained a sufficiently prominent position in the school to 'go into stick-ups'—in other words, to exchange the low collar worn by the majority for some kind of high collar. If anyone was rash enough to adopt this more distinguished kind of neck-gear before he was important enough to justify the change, his friends put him in his place by tearing the collar off and confiscating all the offending articles that they could find in his room. Now there is a tradition known to all boys as to what position in the school or what athletic successes give a right to this form of distinction. There are no rules on these subjects as far as masters are concerned—at any rate there is no written or printed code of law on such points. But there is an etiquette about each matter which is far more effective than any legislation. Efforts on the part of the higher authorities to interfere have usually met with scant success. The public opinion of the school has nearly always been extraordinarily sound in the view taken of what is and what is not in good taste. When common sense dictates an alteration, it either comes from the boys or, if imposed by authority, it is accepted without demur. An instance of the former is provided by the account given by John Maude (see p. 32) of the introduction of greatcoats. 'After a little pressure', he writes, 'we persuaded the authorities that greatcoats and cold baths ought not to be forbidden or discouraged. What the absolute rule about greatcoats was I never could discover, but it was not until 1867 that any general change of custom took place.' He proceeds to describe his own coat, made by Markham of Rugby—where he lived—'of a very close smooth box cloth, of a dark olive green tint, not too green, just graciously hinting at that colour, just avoiding black', and says that he was one of the pioneers in the use of ordinary overcoats such as could be worn in the holidays as well as at school.

Coats of this description, however, appear for a good many years to have been confined to the more prominent boys, the rank and file wearing what was known as a 'woolly bear'—a rough coat of some fluffy material, admirably serviceable, but towards the close of last century becoming unpopular because it was no longer fashionable outside Eton.

An instance of the ready acceptance of a change imposed by authority occurred later. Dr. Warre was perturbed one cold summer at the sight of scores of little boys boating or sitting on the river bank with nothing on but a thin pair of flannel trousers and a rowing zephyr, because the old tight-fitting blue jersey was ill-adapted for rowing. He had but to mention his misgivings to the Captain of the Boats, and an hour or two later a notice appeared in Spottiswoode's—or was it then Ingalton Drake's?— window announcing that from that day forth all boys might wear the ordinary white sweater which had hitherto been the peculiar privilege of Upper Boats. But, though various campaigns have been instituted against the fancy waistcoats of 'Pop', waistcoats are still, if anything, fancier than ever, because the majority of boys and masters agree that, if the rising generation of to-day likes to indulge in the harmless foibles that pleased the rising generation of yesterday and many a day before, it really does not matter.

Various minor changes have of course taken place. In 1911 soft shirts, which, wholly unknown in the last quarter of the previous century, had for some few years been the jealously guarded privilege of 'Pop',

were, in deference to the importance attached by
Dr. Lyttelton to hygienic considerations, legitimised
for all and at once adopted by the great majority.
At the time, however, this alteration was far less conspicuous than, owing to the gradual enlargement of the
opening of the waistcoat, it has since become. To what
cause is to be attributed the sudden abandonment a
year or two later of the almost universal boot in favour
of the now equally universal shoe it is impossible to
say for certain. Bicycling, golf, the disappearance of
mud from the streets of Eton and elsewhere may any
or all of them have contributed to the change.

This Eton costume from the time of its origin up
to fifty years ago and later was far less conspicuous
than it is now, since, with the exception of the white
tie, it was simply the ordinary dress of society. As
this is no longer the case, it is more liable to criticism
from the visitors who now flock to Eton in enormously
increased numbers on any day of the week and at all
hours. Some think that the modern Etonian is less
smartly turned out than his predecessors, but this is
an opinion that can be neither proved nor disproved.
One thing is, however, indisputable, namely that the
adoption of dark trousers has rendered the appearance
of boys seen in the mass, as in Chapel or at Absence,
almost unduly sombre.

The clothes worn for games have also been gradually
modified. Football up to about 1875 was played in
any old pair of trousers that the player happened to
think past ordinary use, while till about the same
date boys on their way to their game were expected

to wear the regulation black tail-coat or Eton jacket. During the following decade these trousers were more and more frequently cut down and made into knickerbockers with a strap and buckle below each knee and another behind the back. Between 1870 and 1880 grey flannel came into fashion and was substituted for the cloth trousers or knickerbockers of earlier generations. But even in the early nineties a well-known mathematical master caused a sensation by appearing on the Field to play against the school clad in an old pair of his black clerical trousers, though the amusement of the spectators was soon changed to amazement and admiration as they saw those black trousers go racing down the ground at a pace which outstripped the fleetest of the school football eleven.

The introduction of grey flannel was followed between 1880 and 1890 by the adoption of shorts instead of knickerbockers. At first the wearing of shorts was purely optional. Later it became the privilege of comparatively few boys who represented their house in the matches for the football cup. Since 1932 this restriction has ceased to exist, and boys who have played for their house without gaining their house colours are distinguished only by house-colour tops to their stockings.

In the Easter Half the only changes in costume to be noted are the adoption by beaglers in general of a uniform, which began to come into fashion in 1891, its main features being breeches and a stock ; and by the Master and Whips of a brown velveteen coat and huntsman's cap. The coat came into use in 1879, the cap in 1893. In the interests of economy various attempts have been made to return to the old system under which boys ran in the same sort of kit that they already possessed for football. But, though there is now nothing to prevent it, there are few, if any, bold enough to appear at a meet in any but the recognised beagling costume.

The dress of earlier beaglers is described in the Memoirs quoted on p. 214, the author of which, after mentioning that the College Beagles before the amalgamation of 1867 were kept 'at Ward's Lodge at the Datchet Lane end of the Playing Fields', continues :

'I have very pleasant memories of early meets at Salt Hill at about eight in the morning', which began with a substantial breakfast at 'Bonham's Hotel'[1] . . . 'I should like to record that our dress for this sport and also for football was deplorably untidy. Grey flannels, shorts, breeches, etc., were of course unknown. Our plan (and this applies not only to College but to the whole school) was to set apart one or two pairs of old morning trousers, and to go on wearing them to the end of the Half. They were never cleaned, and were soon caked with mud. Nor do I remember that our football boots were ever cleaned unless special request was made.'

In the Summer Half, except for the extension in the use of white sweaters already mentioned and the substitution of shorts for trousers on the river owing

---

[1] Every whole holiday was what would now be called a 'non-dies', *i.e.* there was no early school. Chapel was at 3 P.M.

to the introduction of slides, the only change has been in the character of the headgear. Up to the beginning of the present century boys wore either caps or straw hats of the kind now called 'boaters', the latter being confined to those who had passed in swimming. Gradually a felt hat known as a 'land and water' replaced the straw hat, and the latter has now ceased to exist.

These petty details of costume, unimportant as they are in themselves, are nevertheless interesting as an indication of the dislike of boys—and indeed not of boys only—for anything that makes them appear different from their fellows. This attention to little details of etiquette, such as the unwritten law that only members of 'Pop' may carry their umbrellas rolled up, and that the bottom button of the waistcoat must be left unfastened, is part of the innate conservatism of boys. Although it is comic, it has a certain value. It helps to make them conform to type, and, so long as the right type prevails, that is all to the good. As far as can be judged, the rules of convention have become less rigid in recent years, at any rate in cases in which the breach of them is harmless. What would have been the reaction of a past generation to the sight of a smallish boy wheeling a baby brother in a perambulator as he walked up the High Street with his mother and sister? Yet this was seen two or three years ago by one of the authors, and it was noticeable not only that the boy himself showed no sign of embarrassment, but that other boys showed none of surprise.

Another sign of this decrease of self-consciousness is afforded by the Scouts. The smallest boys seem to think it perfectly natural to come into school or Chapel in their Scout dress amongst a crowd of others in ordinary costume. The same phenomenon is also seen in the wearing of uniform whenever circumstances require it. It is now twenty-four years since this concession was first made as regards Chapel.

This allusion to the Corps and the Scouts suggests that some account must be given of what are now two very important institutions.

The early history of the Eton Volunteer Rifle Corps, as it was originally called, was somewhat chequered. It was started by boys, and all the officers and staff from the Captain Commandant downwards were provided by them, though there can be little doubt that Dr. Warre, who came as a temporary master in the Lent Half of 1860, in which year the Corps was founded, had much to do with the movement. The first Captain Commandant was E. W. Chapman, and five out of the six companies formed were commanded by members of the 'Eton Society'. But, as is shown below, the wave of enthusiasm did not last long. The following account of its first ten years is taken from the *E.C.C.* of March 31, 1870 ; it is believed to have been written by Dr. Warre.

'The first Eton Volunteer Corps was formed in the Spring of 1860. The novelty of the undertaking attracted numerous recruits, and ere long the Corps numbered more than 300 members, all belonging to the School. For a short time considerable attention was paid to drill, and when, in 1861, the Eton Volunteers had the honour of being reviewed in Windsor Park by the Queen in person, Her Majesty was pleased to express her approval of their performances, and to ask for a list containing all the names of all the members of the Corps. Rifle shooting also, though carried on under difficulties, was practised with considerable success. The Spencer Cup was won by Etonians in 1861 and 1862, while the Eleven succeeded in carrying off the Ashburton Shield in the following year. Nevertheless the columns of the then nascent *Chronicle* had already begun to teem with letters and admonitory articles on the subject of the declining state of the Rifle Corps. Various attempts were made to resuscitate the military enthusiasm which had once shewn six strong companies on parade, but that enthusiasm had passed away, and the Volunteer service at Eton sank to the level of a mere amusement or employment for the few who chose to embrace it. During the interval which elapsed between the abandonment of the first Corps, and the formation of the second, Eton continued to send a representative shooting Eleven to Wimbledon : but the utmost efforts of certain patriotic Etonians, among whom we may mention the President of the O.U.B.C., failed in obtaining any single success for their School.

'It was accordingly determined, about three years ago, to make an attempt to establish another Volunteer Corps upon a more permanent basis than that of its predecessor. Two reasons in particular had been alleged for the failure of the former institution : first, the difficulty of obtaining competent officers, arising from the fact that the stay of each boy in the Corps was necessarily of short duration ; secondly, the expense and trouble which attended the Shooting : for it was then necessary to drive four miles in order to reach a Rifle Range, where target practice could be obtained. It will be seen, that the second Volunteer Corps was framed specially to meet these objections.

'A sufficient number of gentlemen, resident at Eton, kindly consented to form a permanent staff, and Butts were erected near Chalvey, within easy walking distance of the College. Under these improved auspices, the Rifle Corps again sprang into life. It never indeed could vie with the Corps of 1861 in the length of its muster roll, but we can confidently affirm that it attained to a greater degree of efficiency. A double victory at Wimbledon in 1868 attested the improved state of the Rifle practice ; a success which might perhaps have been repeated last year, had not the zeal of the Volunteers already begun to cool. Many of the most active members of the Rifle Corps left the School at last Election, thus making gaps in the ranks which have not since been filled up.'

The main difference between the Corps of 1860 and that of 1867 was that the latter was officered almost entirely by masters. The first Commanding Officer was Mr. Samuel Evans, while Dr. Warre commanded a Cadet Corps composed, presumably, of smaller and younger boys. The Corps was not maintained at a reasonable strength without difficulty, as is proved by appeals in the *E.C.C.* from time to time, but it was never again in danger of extinction. Annual camps became the fashion about 1870. About 1880 it became a full four-company

battalion with a retired regular officer as adjutant.
The first to hold this position was Major P. T. Godsal,
who had himself as a boy been in the first squad that ✗
ever fired on the Chalvey range. He was succeeded
in 1897 by Major W. J. Myers—the donor, among
many other gifts, of the Egyptian collection in the
School Hall and of many of the windows in Lower
Chapel—who left to take part in the South African
war and was killed at once. Major Soltau-Symons
took his place. Then, in 1908, the battalion became
part of the Officers' Training Corps, and the ad-
jutancy was made a three years' appointment held by
officers seconded from the regular army.

Before 1914 it was rather the fashion in some
quarters to laugh at schoolboy soldiers and to deny
their usefulness. Of their value to the country the
proof was given in that year, when many went to
the front with practically no other training than that
received in the O.T.C. But whatever views may have
been held on this point, no one with experience
of boys can have failed to realise the great educational value of the Corps. For boys of the awkward
age between fifteen and seventeen to have to keep
alert to orders, to obey them instantly, to hold themselves upright and move smartly, and, a little later,
to have to give the words of command themselves
and to see that they are properly carried out, all
constitutes an admirable training in quickness of
intelligence and observation ; and an unsuspected
aptitude for these military duties is often found in
boys otherwise undistinguished, who thereby get

opportunities, which might otherwise be denied them, for developing their self-confidence and sense of responsibility. But for schoolboys the benefit of rifle shooting carried to the degree of proficiency required for success at Bisley is far more doubtful. The time required for practice, the objections to any form of violent exercise for those to whom absolute steadiness of hand is essential, and the isolated nature of the pursuit, render rifle shooting almost incompatible with ordinary school life ; while with the growth of mechanisation individual marksman-ship of the most advanced type is with very few exceptions losing its importance even for military purposes.

Though a pioneer in the Volunteer movement, Eton had no Boy Scouts of its own till fully ten years after General Baden-Powell had started the first Scout troops. It was in 1919, on the initiative of Mr. A. B. Ramsay, then Lower Master, and Mr. E. W. Powell, that the first steps were taken ; and by the end of October in that year there were twenty-eight patrols divided between four troops with a total strength of about two hundred and fifty. Most houses now have one patrol and some two, and these compete for various trophies at the end of the Lent Half. There is also occasionally a senior troop of older boys who hope to become Scout Masters, and endeavour to be as useful as they can to other troops in the neighbourhood.

CHAPTER XIII

GAMES AND SPORTS

Their Uses and Abuses

Football, cricket and fives certainly existed by the middle of the eighteenth century, but of their organisation as part of the ordinary daily life of boys at Eton there is little record until the appearance of *The Eton College Chronicle* in 1863. In this year a challenge cup for house football was presented by the Rev. W. Wayte, while Mr. William Johnson had given a similar cup for cricket in 1860. The first race for the House Four Cup (provided by subscription) took place in 1857, but, as *The Eton Boating Book* (1933) and *The Eton Book of the River* (1935) contain all the information obtainable about the history of boating and boat racing at Eton, it is unnecessary to say anything here about rowing, except to point out that from as early as 1800 up to the present date it has been one of the principal pursuits of a large section of the school.

As football is the one form of exercise in which all boys take part except the few excluded on medical grounds, it naturally comes first in an account of Eton games. In the first decade after 1860 the commonest kind of match was apparently a modified house match, *e.g.* two houses played each other 'from Middle' (or Lower) 'Division downwards'. There were also various matches between different parts of the school, much ingenuity being exercised in devising new distinctions. Thus games are recorded between 'The two sides of the Alphabet (A–L and M–Z)', 'The two sides of College' or 'of Chapel' (Organ side and Pulpit side—see Chapter X, p. 172), Boats *v.* no Boats, Pop *v.* no Pop, Shavers *v.* Non-shavers (E. Lyttelton among the former, A. Lyttelton among the latter), Dissyllables *v.* the Rest, Tall *v.* Short at the Wall, Two first Divisions *v.* the School, while two clubs are mentioned with the picturesque names of 'The Step-and-fetch-its' and 'The Puff-wheeze and gasps'.

It was in this decade that football colours were invented. Apart from the light blue of the Eight and the Eleven there were previously no colours except those of the Boats. The first football colour was that for the School Field eleven, dating from 1860. Two years later this was followed by the introduction of house football colours. No house could claim a right to such colours without the permission of the Captain of the Boats, though, once this permission was given, it rested with the captain of house football to settle which members of the house should be allowed to wear them. Nowadays the number of boys who are allowed to wear their house colours in any house is to some extent regulated by the Keepers of the Field.

Though football to the vast majority of Etonians denotes the Field game, played on a ground of which the correct dimensions have fairly lately been established at 130 by 90 yards, it must be remembered that there is a second game played on a strip of ground five or six yards wide, bounded on one side by a high brick wall. The latter, however, is practically confined to the Collegers, who play it from their earliest days at Eton, and two or three dozen of the older and stronger Oppidans. This explains why the annual contest on St. Andrew's Day between Collegers and Oppidans at the Wall is not such a one-sided affair as the disparity in their respective numbers might suggest.

To return to the Field game, the system of matches between houses, or parts of houses, has not changed essentially between 1860 and the present day, though there has been some alteration in the nomenclature ; for instance, what used to be called a match from Middle (or Lower) Division downwards is now known as a 'Sine'—an abbreviation for *sine coloribus* denoting all who have not yet got their house football colours. The great transformation that has taken place is in what may be called the ordinary, everyday football of those who are not good enough to play in the School Field games, for which sides are selected from the best twenty or thirty players in the school. Up to about 1890 houses were divided into groups, each group containing three or four houses. Every day the captain of football put up a sheet of paper on which all who intended to play football 'after twelve' (*i.e.* between the end of the last morning school and dinner at 2 P.M.) entered their names. The best player, in Eton language the 'highest in choices', of those on the list took this paper with him to the football field, where he met the representatives of the other houses in his group with similar lists. The two highest 'choices' then picked up sides for the first game, and, if there were enough players present, the process was repeated for a second, and sometimes for a third game. Though nothing depended on the result of these games, they were most keenly contested, and, as all the players were of more or less equal calibre, they provided an excellent training in the spirit and theory of the game.

But about 1890 the idea of taking part in any athletic pursuit merely for the pleasure it afforded began to yield to the competitive spirit. In the earlier days the football or cricket that boys played consisted for three-quarters of the Half of these pick-up games, and they rowed up to Surly or Monkey, often as hard as they could, without any idea of training for a race. Indeed, except for lower boy races which only concerned two or three dozen boys, there were no races for them to train for until they got into the Boats. This was no longer enough. In football the pick-up games just mentioned were gradually replaced by house matches. At first these were played against various scratch sides, largely composed of masters, and this tended to improve the standard of play, as it happened that in the decade between 1893 and 1903 there were several outstanding football players among the newcomers on the staff. Matters continued without much change till the war.

Then, owing to the absence of all the younger able-bodied members of the staff, the system of scratch matches broke down, and the boys took to playing house matches against one another. Now the influence of the war has begun to weaken and, though matches between houses are still common, scratches are again becoming more numerous. About 1920 a cup was given for a new competition, called the House Second Eleven or House Second Sine Cup, for which boys who have not played for their house are eligible. There are also two competitions between houses, one for all lower boys, the Final of which is played on St. Andrew's Day, and one for boys under fourteen and a half years of age. The last three weeks of the Half are devoted to the latter and to the matches for the House Football Cup, perhaps the most coveted trophy in the school.

With the age and origin of cricket this book is not concerned, but it may be of interest to note in passing that the game was popular as far back as the time of Horace Walpole (1736), and that the earliest match recorded in which Etonians took part was in 1751, when Eton College, Past and Present, played the Gentlemen of England in three matches lasting from June 25 to 29, winning one and losing two of the matches. As these were played at Newmarket, the present Etonians must surely have been a figment of the reporter's imagination. A fact that seems curious to our ideas is that various other sports were going on simultaneously, including football matches, at one of which there were six thousand spectators.

The three cricket matches are said to have been played for a stake of £1,500.[1]

Up to comparatively recent times the great handicap to cricket at Eton was the shortage of grounds. But before this is discussed, something must be said for the benefit of those not familiar with Eton of the various names that will occur. They are mostly used in two senses, denoting firstly the ground, and secondly the group of boys who play on it.

Geographically Sixpenny, *alias* the Field, *alias* the Timbralls, is the field lying between the Slough Road and the Fives Courts. The name Sixpenny is due to the fact that in 1830 a club for lower boys was started for which the subscription was sixpence.

On the other side of the Slough Road is College Field. Up to 1863 this was used by Collegers for an upper and a lower game. In that year an amalgamation took place between the Lower College game and Lower Club. A new club was formed, under the name of Middle Club, composed of the better players in the two old games, while the inferior players of both constituted the new Lower Club and played in the Triangle.

The Triangle is a field bounded on the west by an avenue of elms, and on the east by the path from Sheep's Bridge to Datchet Lane. It was enlarged to its present size and shape in 1863, when the path was raised and made to run, as now, nearer the river. Later the Middle Club game was brought to this ground and Lower Club moved to College Field.

---

[1] *Etoniana*, R. A. Austen-Leigh, No. 8.

Between the elm avenue just mentioned and the Slough Road lies Upper Club.

In 1863—and indeed up to as late as 1886—the only cricket grounds available were those in Upper Club, the Triangle, College Field and Sixpenny, about thirteen acres in all. Even to-day complaints are often heard of the danger caused by the undue proximity of those playing at nets or in games, and these complaints certainly seem to have not a little justification. A letter in the *Chronicle* of July 2, 1863, gives a vivid picture of the scene in Sixpenny in those days and is worth quoting in full.

'May I call attention through your columns', asks the writer, 'to the dangerous way in which games and matches are carried on in Sixpenny? The other night I was playing a match on that ground, and there were no less than seven other matches going on at the same time in the same field, and placing one's life in continual jeopardy. Surely it is the business of the two "Keepers" to see about this; and although one belongs to "Upper Club" and will most probably be in the "Eleven", is there any reason why the other should not, besides collecting subscriptions for Sixpenny, go round every evening to see that all is right; he ought *never* to let *more* than four matches be played there at the same time, as the ground is not large enough, especially as there are many other fellows practising in the field at the same time as the matches are being played.'

Such letters recur with considerable regularity, and with good reason. Anyone who frequented the cricket grounds, especially Sixpenny, before 1890 will remember the frequent cry of 'Thank you, cut over !' —a polite way of requesting that a boy who had just been struck on the head, body or leg by a ball hit at random by one of the many playing stump cricket on the edge of the ground should return it to the striker.

Among the other games of cricket that took place in this confined area was one now extinct—house cricket sweepstakes. There were two a side ; runs could only be made in front of the wicket ; the batsman's partner kept wicket ; the other side bowled and fielded as they could. For this event practically the whole house entered, and, as they were divided into strokes and bows, the best and worst performers, matches were often very keen, huge scores were made, and the condition of the players at the end of a hot summer's day was not far removed from that of Quanko Samba as described by Mr. Jingle.

Up to about 1850 the fields known afterwards, first as Upper and Lower Club, and now as Upper Club and the Triangle, were called the Upper and Lower Shooting Fields. This name dates back at any rate to the time of Queen Elizabeth, as there is an entry in the Eton Audit Book (1600) of a payment for making 'a waye by the shooting fild at the Quenes being here' (Maxwell-Lyte). It may be conjectured that they were used for archery and that the terms upper and lower referred to their level. Hence, probably, the names Upper and Lower Club. Middle Club, as shown above, is a later creation.

In 1887 there was some reorganisation of games which relieved the pressure on Sixpenny by moving one game to Jordan and one, for boys under fourteen, to the apex of the Triangle ; and in 1888 the Lower Boy Cricket Cup became the Junior Cricket Cup. In 1889 a field of four or five acres was brought into use and christened Mesopotamia. But it was the purchase of Agar's Plough in 1894–5 that changed the whole situation. In that year it was discovered that a building syndicate had bought a large portion of the frontage of Chalvey field, between the Slough Road and the Great Western line. Some masters and Old Etonians subscribed £6,000 to buy out the syndicate ; and this enabled them to rouse the College to the necessity of acquiring the rest of Chalvey field and the whole of Agar's Plough—the land bounded by the Slough Road, Upton Park, the Myrke, and Datchet Lane. The twelve acres purchased by Old Etonians were presented to College 'unconditionally, but on the honourable understanding that the land should never be built upon'.[1] The area of Chalvey field is about 90 acres ; that of Agar's Plough 120.

Agar's Plough, which had been nearly all arable land, was converted to grass and partially levelled. In 1898 two large cricket grounds, now known as Agar's Plough and Dutchman's Farm respectively, were opened on it, and the same year saw the institution of junior cricket matches, a series of league matches for boys under sixteen played between houses in two

[1] *E.C.C.*, May 7, 1903.

groups and ending in a final between the winners of each group. The old Lower Sixpenny colours were also abolished this year.

Previously, except for the House Cricket Cup, played towards the end of the Half, and the Junior Cricket Cup, cricket at Eton was based on the club games. The junior matches under the new system only affected the two lowest of these, alternate weeks being allotted to juniors and club games. But in 1921 a series of friendly matches between house elevens took away a certain number of days from the other clubs. In 1934 the character of these matches was altered, and the House Cricket Cup was played on much the same system as the junior matches, houses being divided into four groups and the two best in each group going on to play for the Cup after Lord's. In the last year or two a further development on the same lines has been effected by the creation of a middle league, consisting of those who are neither juniors nor members of the house cricket eleven.

The resulting organisation is less complicated than this historical survey makes it appear. Side by side there are two units—the house and the club. At no point do they come in contact with one another. The house has three cricket elevens, or more often two and a bit. These are the house cricket eleven, the junior cricket eleven, and the middle league eleven, the last usually a combination of two houses, as, owing to the counter-attractions of the river, few houses have material for three full elevens.

For the houses there are two cricket cups—the House Cricket Cup and the Junior Cricket Cup, both, as already mentioned, beginning on the league system and ending with one or more rounds of a knock-out competition. The league portion of each is so arranged that house and junior matches never clash with one another. The object of the Middle League is to provide moderate players with a more attractive alternative than a constant succession of mere games.

The clubs are arranged quite independently of houses. They are Upper Club, Second Upper Club, Lower Club, Upper Sixpenny and Lower Sixpenny. The two first-named contain the three best elevens in the school, regardless of age or position. The boys playing in them vary constantly, so that all who are sufficiently promising may have a chance of showing what they can do. Lower Club is confined to boys in Fifth Form under seventeen ; Upper Sixpenny to those in Fifth Form under sixteen ; and Lower Sixpenny to lower boys.

Each club is divided into two or three games or more, according to the number of players available. There are also a few club matches, either between two clubs or against an outside team.

For coaching purposes there are house and junior nets, arranged by the captain of cricket in each house ; and club nets, arranged by the keeper of each club.

There are no house cricket colours, but besides the Eleven and the Twenty-two—*i.e.* the first and second elevens—the best eleven players in Second Upper Club, Lower Club and Upper Sixpenny, respectively, receive distinctive colours.

For greater convenience in the organisation of their games, the first afternoon school for lower boys does not coincide with that of upper boys.

Apart from football, cricket and the river there are many other outdoor pursuits. The claims of cricket, rowing and football in the summer and winter relegate these mainly, but not exclusively, to the Lent schooltime. The first place is taken by fives, which employs more boys than any other single game played in that Half. Before 1870 the opportunities in this direction were limited to some eight or ten courts and the Chapel buttresses, but after that date courts increased very rapidly, and the number is now seven or eight times as great, numerous competitions have sprung up, and there are cups for School Fives, House Fives, Junior Fives, Junior House Fives, and, in the Christmas Half, Lower Boy House Fives.

Probably the Beagles rank next after fives in point of antiquity, though the exact date at which the Collegers started the first pack known at Eton is uncertain. A rival pack was got up by the Oppidans in 1857, and ten years later the two amalgamated. The *Chronicle*, in commenting on this amalgamation, says that 'in order to prevent too numerous a field turning out, the number of subscribers will be limited to 70'. Till 1899 the pack had no kennels of its own. For a quarter of a century or more before that date they were kept by one Lock behind his Turkish Bath establishment in what are now the back premises of the School Stores stationery department—No. 7 High Street. In that year the energy of the twin brothers, Francis and Riversdale Grenfell, led to the building of the present kennels just beyond the ditch east of Agar's Plough. In old days the pack was a very scratch affair composed of hounds of all sizes and speeds. It is now a model of uniformity and will bear comparison with any ; but owing to the variety of other attractions and the large increase in costs of all kinds since the war its financial position is not as satisfactory as might be wished. This shortage of money makes it impossible to remove an obstacle which, by diminishing the country available for hunting, tends to lessen the attraction of the sport. The electrification of the Southern Railway between Staines and Windsor has rendered it impossible to take hounds into that neighbourhood. For five or six hundred pounds fencing could be put up which would obviate this difficulty, and this would be to the benefit not only of the E.C.H., but of all those living in the neighbourhood who have children or pet animals. It is much to be hoped that some way may be found of restoring the pack to its old footing. Its disappearance would be a misfortune, for not only does it provide occupation and exercise for a number of boys who have no taste for ball games and no aptitude for athletics, but it is the only form of recreation that takes them outside the square mile or so to which their other pursuits are limited, and therefore the only one that develops their sense of direction and eye for country.

As regards athletic sports there is not much to be said. 'The oldest of the School races is the Steeple-chase, which seems to have been run first in '47. The races known as the School mile, Quarter mile, Hundred yards, and Hurdles were inaugurated in '56, and the Walking race in '66, this last being discontinued in '96 and the Half mile substituted. The High jump, the Long jump, Throwing the cricket-ball, the Weight, and the Hammer are all first recorded in '65' (Gambier-Parry). Some at any rate of the last group owe their origin to the Master of the Beagles, who in 1862 used his surplus to provide prizes for them, a better use for it than was made by his successor a couple of years later, who spent it on a breakfast to subscribers and wine for the Boats. Up to 1888 the different races were scattered over the Christmas and Lent schooltimes. They were all under the control of the Captain of the Boats, who had no assistance in the arrangements for them beyond what he could obtain from voluntary helpers. In that year Lord Ampthill, in his second year as Captain of the Boats, instituted the Athletic Committee to form an official advisory body for all matters connected with the sports. It was settled that the races and sports should all take place in the Lent school-time and as far as possible on one day ; and in 1889 this arrangement was carried out for the first time, and has continued practically unchanged to the present date. The only innovations of any importance have been the introduction of a half-mile race and a house relay race ; boys under fourteen and a half have also recently competed in a class by themselves for certain events. There are also two challenge cups, one for the house, the other for the individual gaining the greatest number of points. In 1880 a tug of war was instituted, the sides that year being chosen from dames and tutors. In 1881 wetbobs *v.* drybobs was substituted, but the wetbobs proved so far superior that in 1882 and 1883 the old distinction of north and south was experimentally revived. After this the contest settled down to its present form of wetbobs *v.* drybobs.

Other amusements in the Lent Half have at various times included rackets, association and Rugby football, hockey, fencing, boxing, jiu-jitsu, gymnastics, golf, lawn tennis on hard courts, and paperchases.

To take the minor items in this list first, a letter in the *Chronicle* from the Rev. A. G. L'Estrange proves that hockey was flourishing between 1840 and 1850, with an upper and lower club and regular keepers. It was then rapidly superseded by football, and except for an outburst in 1868 which does not seem to have lasted more than a year, has never been revived.

Fencing and boxing are old institutions at Eton, as elsewhere, but their present popularity probably dates back to the building of the gymnasium in 1907. It was, of course, not till after this that jiu-jitsu and gymnastics became possible. Golf and lawn tennis are not confined to the Lent Half, but the former flourishes then more than at other times. Paper-chases have never concerned any but the smaller boys and seem of late years almost to have disappeared.

Two racket courts were built in 1868, but owing to expense the game has always been limited to a comparatively small number. Since the end of last century squash has gained ground rapidly. In rackets there are various competitions, both single and double, and squash is beginning to develop along the same lines.

Association football was played by Eton boys at any rate as long ago as 1865, for in that year *The Field* has a description, rather complimentary to the boys, of a match at Battersea Park between the school and the Civil Service. The popularity of the game has ebbed and flowed, and at times it has been completely dropped. Rugby, though a later comer— it only started after the beginning of this century— has obtained a firmer hold on the school, and there is now a school side with a colour of its own, while seven-a-side matches between houses rouse a good deal of enthusiasm.

Enthusiastic advocates of the Rugby game sometimes urge that it should replace the Eton field game on the ground that Etonians would thus have more chance of distinction as University or international players, and that such a change would make it possible for matches to be arranged against other schools and might lead to a league competition culminating 'in a Public School Rugby Final to be played annually at Twickenham'. This is what a correspondent of the *Chronicle*, signing himself 'Twickenham', prayed three years ago that he might 'live to see'. To this aspiration no better answer is possible than that given by Mr. A. O. Van Oss in the following number of the *Chronicle*, of which the last paragraph must be quoted in full.

'It should be remembered', he writes, 'that serious Rugby is as great a strain as serious cricket or serious rowing. A Lent Half in which games are played almost exclusively for enjoyment has always seemed, perhaps especially strongly to a non-Etonian, to be one of Eton's most precious liberal institutions, which should be maintained at all costs. May "Twickenham" never "live to see Eton in a Public School final", and may he live to a ripe old age.'

The attitude towards games revealed by 'Twickenham's' letter has already done much harm. For a boy to wish to attain the highest degree of proficiency of which he is capable in his recreations as well as in his work is a natural and healthy ambition. If this ambition leads to the desire to prove his school superior to others in any particular direction, there is no sort of objection to friendly contests such as already exist, many of them hallowed by long tradition. But that these should be multiplied and become the subject of exaggerated effusions in the daily papers is deplorable. The undue publicity given nowadays to schoolboy games may well end by making the players lose all sense of proportion. If this tendency is not checked, boys at school will in a few decades be divided into those who play cricket, those who row, those who run or jump or throw the discus, those who play football or fives or rackets or even squash, and those who work ; and, as is already largely the case in the United States, their whole training and energy will be directed to one single pursuit, as though that were the only aim of life. Under such a system recreation, as an essential element in education, will cease to exist, and professionalism will destroy that balance between mental and physical qualities and that deep-rooted sense of values which has helped to make English public schools the envy of not a few other nations.

CHAPTER XIV

SIDELINES AND SOCIETIES

A wealth of Interests

At Eton, as elsewhere, there are certain institutions which fall under no particular heading, but yet play a considerable part in the life of the school. These include undertakings managed gratuitously by masters for the benefit and with the participation of boys, such as the School Stores and Laundry, and the Book Pound. Of the Eton College Boat House and Queen's Eyot so full an account has been recently given in *The Eton Book of the River* that further mention of them here would be superfluous.

SCHOOL STORES

The School Stores were founded in 1900 on the initiative of the Rev. Lionel Ford, afterwards Headmaster of Repton and Harrow, and Dean of York. The first step was the purchase of the business which had hitherto been run by 'Joby' Powell, and, when he became bedridden, by his son and son-in-law. Here in a rickety old shed were sold 'sock', fives balls and gloves, cricket bats and balls, footballs and such other articles as boys required for their games, while old Powell also superintended the marking out of football grounds and provided the balls for the Field and Wall. This shed was almost immediately replaced by a small brick building, which survived for a quarter of a century, after which the whole site was laid out afresh to allow of the completion of the row of covered courts.

The next stage began when in 1904 the management of 'Little Brown's', *alias* 'Bunker's', was taken over. This was followed in course of time by the gradual absorption of another 'sock' shop on the school side of Barnes Pool. Up to 1920 no further developments occurred, the School Stores confining its attention to 'sock' and such athletic goods as could be conveniently supplied from the Fives Courts branch.

After the war there came a change of policy. The first important step towards the subsequent expansion was the acquisition in 1922 of the School Laundry Company's business and property. Almost simultaneously Mat Wright,[1] wishing to retire from the business that he had built up, offered it to the School Stores on very generous terms, and himself continued to help with this side of the business. By 1926 what had been known to many Old Etonians as 'Merrick's' had become the silversmith's and watchmaking branch of the School Stores, and there were also departments for boots and shoes, grocery and stationery, while 'Webber's', or, later, 'Rowland's', the only 'sock' shop at Barnes Pool that had not been

[1] Engaged by Mr. R. A. H. Mitchell in the early nineties as a cricket professional and authorised to open a shop for the supply of bats and the usual accessories of cricket and other games.

previously acquired, was taken over and an extensive new restaurant added at the back.

At this juncture the School Stores had to face a violent attack on the part of a small but influential section of the staff, who for a variety of reasons disapproved of the whole movement. This led to an enquiry by the College authorities, who were alarmed by the rapidity of the recent expansion and doubtful of the financial position. Their investigation, while establishing beyond question the soundness of the finance and the correctness of the methods of management, ended in the framing of a new constitution which gave the Stores a legal entity.

After 1926 the School Stores suffered with all other businesses from the universal depression, and all idea of further expansion had to be abandoned for the time being. Up to this point the whole burden of management had rested on some twelve or fifteen masters, whose only possible time for a committee meeting was at 10 P.M. after a long day's work, when the prospect of early school at 7.30 A.M. next morning tended to limit the time available for discussion. Under them was a paid manager. Sergeant-Major Rushworth, on his retirement from the Corps, held this position for many years. While the School Stores was a comparatively simple organisation this arrangement worked well. The attempt was then made to combine the office of manager with that of school clerk. Captain A. C. Baker for some time managed to fill the dual position most efficiently ; but, when the seven branches mentioned above had come into being, it became obvious that a whole-time manager was essential.

In 1933 such a manager was found in the person of Major R. M. Buckley, M.C., who had been Captain of the Boats in 1913. Two years later he left to take up other work, and was succeeded by Mr. T. H. Wallis, also an Old Etonian. Under this new system the School Stores is in a fair way to recover all, and more than all, the prosperity of the best years before the depression.

BOOK POUND

The Book Pound, an institution founded by Dr. Warre exactly fifty years ago, receives books left about in school or elsewhere at the end of each Half, sorts them, and exhibits them for sale at prices ranging from 2d. to 1s., or possibly in rare cases a trifle more. The greatest bargain on record in its history thus far is the purchase from it by one of the staff of a first edition of *Paradise Lost* for the former sum and its subsequent sale for several thousand times that price.

The Pound is useful in two ways : it enables boys or masters rapidly to replace any missing book, and it provides a store from which the latter can purchase cheaply or borrow gratuitously sets of books for use in school or pupil-room. This collection was until recently kept at the school office and managed by the school clerk, but is now housed in the stationery department of the School Stores.

SCHOOL HALL

The building of the School Hall and Library, with the subsequent additions and alterations made, have already been mentioned (see p. 190). The idea of a hall in which he could address the whole school had been cherished by Dr. Warre from the beginning of his headmastership, but the occasion for an appeal to Old Etonians for money to provide such a building did not occur till after the South African war. It may be worth while to put upon record two facts not generally known about this subject. Dr. Warre's wish was to have two storeys, the upper of which might contain a really good set of rooms for 'Pop', similar accommodation for Sixth Form, and a reading room in connection with the Library. Unluckily, however, the committee of taste appointed to settle details selected a plan which contained no upper floor. The committee then proceeded, with results that they themselves probably learnt later to regret, to insist on drastic modifications of the architect's plan. Briefly stated, the difference between the original design and the form that it eventually took is that in the first the hall was intended to stand with its side parallel to the street and the domed library behind it. The latter would not have been seen from the front, but when viewed from the Dorney Road the Hall and Library would have formed an harmonious group. The present arrangement was imposed on the architect by the committee ; and the elaboration of the present front is the result of

247   R

his attempt to adapt an inconspicuous part of his scheme to a position for which it was not intended.

It seems curious to those who to-day read the accounts of the early discussions about the School Hall, to find how general was the assumption among both supporters and opponents of the scheme that little use would be made of it, the former urging that it was an essential part of such a memorial that it should have no utilitarian value, the latter objecting to it on the ground that it would serve no practical purpose.

That the Hall has proved a worthy memorial none will deny. Of its constant usefulness a few instances may be given.

Besides providing room for examinations for which no adequate provision has been made elsewhere, and for meetings of importance to the neighbourhood such as those of the Windsor and Eton Choral Society and the local branch of the Workers' Educational Association, the Hall contains an organ, a permanent stage for the production of Shakespearean and French plays, a permanent fireproof installation for cinema lectures, and tiers of seats at the back of the stage for concerts and orchestral performances. It seats about a thousand people, and has proved invaluable in the afternoon of a wet Fourth of June when the Guards' band has been transferred to it from the Playing Fields. In it recent portraits of interest to Etonians are placed in dignified surroundings. And so in the space of thirty years the School Hall has become a real centre of school life.

SOCIETIES

Of societies the oldest and best known is that of which the official title is 'The Eton Society', though universally known as 'Pop'. This started as a social club and debating society in the year 1811. In its early days it met at a 'sock' shop called Hatton's and its alternative name is said to be an abbreviation of the Latin word *popina*, meaning a cook-shop. Though debates have been occasionally held in comparatively recent times, the character of the society has changed, and election to it now depends chiefly on athletic distinction and good fellowship. In 1899 a new principle was introduced as the result of a broad hint from Dr. Warre, who, when new rooms were needed owing to the imminent demolition of the old ones, suggested that a society once known as the Literati had deviated from its original tradition by electing boys comparatively low down in the school. The boys responded by making a rule that a certain number of Sixth Form, including the Captain of the School and the Captain of the Oppidans, should be made members *ex officio*, but the total number remained twenty-eight as before.

Originally 'Pop' had no responsibility. Indeed John Maude[1] in his Memoirs mentions that in 'a sock shop close to Barnes Pool Bridge, kept by a man also named Barnes', there was 'an inner sanctum' the use of which was confined to a privileged ten or twelve boys, who formed a kind of 'Privy Council', and

[1] See p. 32.

exercised a wholly unofficial jurisdiction, which the writer considered superior to that of 'Pop'. Of the latter he expressly says that it had not then nearly as much power as now.

For some seventy years, however, this society has exercised an authority which, at first unofficial, has been more and more largely recognised in the course of the present century. The extent of this authority and the dividing line between it and the control of masters is quite undefined. But an arrangement that enables the Headmaster, and in a minor degree assistant masters, to discuss with a self-elected body of boys such difficulties as may from time to time arise is of undoubted value. The superiority of this institution, the independence of which is peculiarly characteristic of Eton, over a prefectorial or monitorial system, lies in the fact that the members of the Eton Society are chosen by boys and not by the Headmaster.

Of other societies there have been many; their names are self-explanatory. The chief of these are now :

The Archaeological Society.

The Essay Society.

The Film Society.

The Gramophone Society.

The Natural History Society.

The Photographic Society.

The Political Society.

The Scientific Society.

The Shakespeare Society.

Le Cercle français.

BIRD SANCTUARY

The nature of the Thames valley renders it a favourite haunt for birds, and the absence of enclosed properties and the freedom from rules as to bounds enables boys to roam over the country round Eton at will. As long ago as 1868 a very remarkable book on the birds of Berkshire and Buckinghamshire was produced by A. W. M. Clark-Kennedy, then a boy of sixteen at Eton. He records that at that time two hundred and twenty-five different species of birds could be found in the neighbourhood as 'visitors' or 'residents', though eighty of these are described as 'rare and accidental'. The study of bird-life has had its individual votaries among boys and masters at all periods ; but not till it fortunately happened that Mr. M. D. Hill, Mr. H. M. Bland, author of *Birds in an Eton Garden*, and Mr. A. Mayall were at Eton together as members of the staff was any attempt made to impart to a larger number of boys the expert knowledge that these three possessed. Gradually there arose a demand, strongly backed by Mr. E. W. Powell, for a bird sanctuary. About a year after his death the Natural History Society took the matter up, a part of the osier bed at Hester's Shed was put at their disposal, and this has now been fenced off and is being put into better order as rapidly as funds permit.

DEBATING SOCIETIES

When debates ceased to be a chief function of 'Pop' a school Debating Society was started, but does not appear to have flourished very long. There are debating societies in most houses, but their activity naturally varies with the character of the leading boys in each house.

PICTURE GALLERY

This has already been mentioned in connection with the Drawing Schools. It is used for exhibitions of the work of different periods, loan collections, pictures by boys and masters, the holiday task drawings done by boys on set subjects of all kinds, and also for marionette shows in which the scenery, figures and costumes are designed by members of the school.

ETON MISSION

The Eton Mission was founded in 1880 under the auspices of Dr. Hornby and Dr. Warre, with the object of giving boys an interest in some charitable work. The scene chosen for its activities was Hackney Wick, a district in the north-east of London. The Council from the first included all masters, all members of Sixth Form, boys holding other prominent positions in the school and one representative elected by each house. The missioner for the first eleven years was the Rev. W. M. Carter, who subsequently became Archbishop of Cape Town. This is not the place to give details of the early development of the work, which can be found in the *Chronicles* of June 16, 1892, and May 19, 1898.

The chief landmarks in its history are the building of the Mission House in 1889, of the present church, a fine building designed by Messrs. Bodley and Garner, in 1892, and of the Eton House, which provides accommodation for visitors from the school and elsewhere, in 1898. A committee of Old Etonians in London has charge of most of the financial administration.

CHAPTER XV

EPILOGUE

Probably no other profession is the target for so much criticism as that of the schoolmaster. The number of Acts of Parliament that have been passed on the subject of education, the amount written about it in various books and magazines, the Associations and Conferences of Headmasters and Assistant Masters, the publication of an Educational Supplement to *The Times*, might lead the superficial observer to the conclusion that it was one of the chief interests of the whole population. Nothing could be further from the truth. One of the greatest difficulties that a schoolmaster has to contend with is the complete apathy of the vast majority of both young and old as regards the whole business. A father, bringing a son to a public school for his first Half, tells the prospective tutor that he does not expect the boy to be a genius, but that all that matters is that he should be an ordinary, decent sort of man. Mothers impress upon the matron that of course health comes first. Reports of idleness are met with the reply that the parents are sorry that their boy has not done better, but that he is very well and happy, and they are glad to hear that he gets on well with his companions. Eminent statesmen, lawyers or generals, called upon to make speeches to the school on some great occasion, perjure themselves by statements that they never learnt anything at school, that they never rose above the lowest division, but that it always has been, is, and they hope always will be the best of schools. Old members of the school of all ages regale one another with stories, nearly all apocryphal, of the ways in which they outwitted the authorities by methods usually far from creditable. Of course there are many brilliant exceptions, but, as a general rule, it might almost be imagined that the community at large had formed a conspiracy to impress on schoolboys the belief that almost the only thing in their school life that does not matter is their school work.

Nor is the contribution of so-called educationists of any value. Some of these are enthusiasts for particular branches of knowledge, loud in their assertion that theirs is the only subject that has ever been of any use to them and that therefore a large amount of time must be devoted to it in any education worth the name. They forget that the fact that it has appealed to them is no proof that it will appeal equally to all. Others, as a rule excellent teachers themselves, advocate through thick and thin the particular method which they have evolved, not realising in their humility that success in teaching comes not from any peculiarity of method, which indeed, in the hands of a master of his craft, is apt to be varied almost infinitely to meet the requirements of the moment, but from the personality of the individual teacher. It may in fact be taken as almost axiomatic that the more startling the results of a method may be in certain hands, the less suitable will it be found for the ordinary exponent of average class teaching.

This state of indifference on the part of the many and misdirected zeal on the part of the few is deplorable. Schools will never take their rightful place in the general social structure until the ordinary person—in other words the vast majority which forms public opinion and decides the issue of elections —is convinced by personal experience of the desirability of education, not merely to refine manners or to obtain a job, but as an avenue to a fuller life.

And yet those who can measure the changes which have taken place during the past sixty years can see many reasons for hope. Boys may be muddled, they may carry away few really deep and permanent impressions, but with few exceptions they are at any rate occupied, and for the most part interested in something, even if it is not their school work. The hopeless inertia induced among the unfit by the old classical education has disappeared. It remains with the new generation to see that the somewhat aimlessly busy boy of to-day is presented with something to do that will be really worth his while.

If this is to be so, schoolmasters must remember that the real test of their efficiency lies, not in the success of brilliant pupils in winning prizes and scholarships, but in the gradual improvement in mental calibre of boys who in the early stages show no intellectual promise and no desire to learn. It is easy to teach clever boys, and their rapid progress, ending in some scholastic triumph, brings a quick return. But the man who devotes himself to the duller task of hammering on till he is sure that a certain amount of sound knowledge is firmly embedded in less responsive brains will find a more lasting reward in the gratitude of his old pupils.

Finally, it may be worth while to state briefly the conclusions to which their researches into the past have led the authors.

The history of education at Eton, and indeed in England generally, for the last seventy or eighty years is the history of a struggle for the inclusion of an ever-increasing variety of subjects in the ordinary course of training of all young people, whatever their mental capacity and whatever their special gifts. The struggle has been to a large extent successful, and it is this very success that is the main cause of the weakness of present-day education.

The mistake that has been made is that each new subject in turn has been introduced as an addition to those previously taught rather than a substitute for one or other of them. The old classical scholars were right in taking two subjects only and teaching them thoroughly [1]; they were wrong in thinking

[1] How thoroughly may be shown by the case of two men who were boys at school between 1840 and 1850, both being connections of one of the authors. A retired officer in the Guards, as his powers began to fail towards the end, spent his mornings at a big table in the library of his house in Scotland doing Latin verses and cursing the footman

that the two subjects they had chosen were the only ones of any value and that they were suitable for all types of intelligence and at every stage.

The champions of the new order had so strong a case that their assault was irresistible. Public opinion began to change. Its influence made itself felt first in the schools, then in the Universities. But the champions of the old order were too securely entrenched to be entirely ousted. Some compromise had to be found. The result was that Greek was to a large extent dropped, while Latin in a modified form, robbed of most of its background of history and mythology, became a dull, unsatisfactory subject in no way comparable to the former classical education.

It is therefore not greatly to be wondered at if education in this country is at present in no very high repute. The battle for the emancipation of the young from the thraldom of the dead languages was won, not because the dead languages are in themselves a bad medium of education, but because they are not an appropriate diet for all. As has already been said, a boy who is physically healthy and vigorous, with the appetite of a wolf and the digestion of an ostrich, thrives on any food, however solid. But this is no argument for inflicting similar fare on the many whose stomachs turn against such nourishment.

It might be imagined that after so recent a demon-

employed to look out words in the Gradus. Another man of about equal mental calibre, whose lot was cast in London, used to take his Eton Horace with him to read in the train, even in the sulphurous atmosphere of the unelectrified Underground.

stration of this truth a new generation would avoid falling into the same error. But the fact is far otherwise. We have escaped from one form of tyranny only to be threatened with another, and that a worse one. The classics were at any rate both linguistic and literary, and therefore fulfilled to a large extent the requirements of true education. Science and mathematics are neither. For purely utilitarian reasons a modicum of arithmetic is an essential part of the equipment required to enable a boy to face the world. But algebra and theoretical geometry are of no more use to the vast majority than Latin and Greek, and they do not provide nearly so good a preliminary training. Science, except for a working knowledge of its practical results, is of little greater value to those who have no special aptitude for it.

Why then should we expect the youth of to-day, after being rescued from one Procrustean bed, to lie upon another? Having convinced ourselves that it is not good that all alike should learn Latin and Greek, why should we now ordain that none may be exempted from science or mathematics, or any other subject or subjects in the world? Even if it be admitted that for a fair number science, and for a smaller number moderately advanced mathematics, may provide an adequate training—which has still to be proved—this is no argument for their retention in anything like their present form in the education of the vast majority.

These remarks are not intended as an attack on Latin or Greek, science or mathematics, or any other particular subject. The point that has to be emphasised again and again, and on which it is impossible to dwell too strongly, is that boys of only moderate intelligence cannot tackle with success more than two, or at most three, main subjects, and that those subjects which do not come in this category must be taught in such a way as to arouse the maximum of interest with the minimum expenditure of time and energy. The main subjects should be approached as something that is to develop habits of thoroughness and accuracy that will last a lifetime ; the minor subjects as something that will enable the learner to take an intelligent interest in the world around him. The former should teach him how to work himself ; the latter how to appreciate the results of the work of others.

Of the truth and importance of these closing words so convinced are the authors that they can but re-echo the prayer of Job :

'Oh that they were graven with an iron pen and lead in the rock for ever !'

Not in Trials Rooms.			C
	Tues. July 14	$11\frac{1}{2}$	Latin Pr
	Mon. July 20	10.20	Fr. U
1	Mon. July 20	$4\frac{1}{2}$	El. Ma
*	Tues. July 21	8	sPrac. S (7.30
2		$10\frac{1}{2}$	Hist. & G
3	Wed. July 22	8	Latin Tra
4		$10\frac{1}{2}$	Science s Physi Lat. Tr C 3
5		$4\frac{1}{2}$	French
6	Thurs. July 23	8	Add. M
7		$10\frac{1}{2}$	Gk. Co h (1) Ess (2) Ma s Chem
8	Fri. July 24	8	Unseen h, s $\frac{1}{2}$ Fre Sent.
9		$10\frac{1}{2}$	El. Matl
10		$4\frac{1}{2}$	Gk. Trs. h Imperial Hist. s Prac. S
11	Sat. July 25	$10\frac{1}{4}$	Verses hr Alts. (1 h
12	Mon. July 27	$7\frac{1}{2}$	Divinity

* Greek Altern

APPENDIX

(containing specimens of the forms mentioned on
pp. 162–164)

P. 262.—Names of masters and number of boys assigned to
each room. *See* p. 162.

P. 263.—Time-table. *See* p. 162.

P. 264.—Names and Trials number of each boy. *See* p. 162.

P. 265.—Rules for invigilation and for dealing with papers
and marks. *See* p. 163.

P. 266.—Rules for boys in Trials, printed on the blotting-
paper supplied for the examination.

P. 267.—Mark sheet. *See* p. 163.

P. 268.—Mark slip, printed on cartridge paper, with the
boy's Trials number stamped in the top right-hand
corner, and his name and his tutor's initials written in
the margin at the top. *See* p. 164.

TRIALS, SUM

Mr. Wilkes,

7 QUEEN'S SCHO
    Mr. Str
HEAD MASTER'S
BALDWIN'S BEC
QUEEN'S   1
SCHOOLS   2
      3
      4
      5
KEATE'S   1
LANE   2
SCIENCE SCHOO
QUEEN'S SCHOO

    W
    M
DRILL   1
HALL   2
SCHOOLS   3
      4
      5
      6
      7
      8
      9
      10
WARRE   1
SCHOOLS   2
      3
      4
      5
      6
      7
      8
NEW   2
SCHOOLS   4
      5
      12
      14
      15
      9
      10
      11
      31
    TRI
Mr. Chute,

C   D
ROOM No. 3, WARRE SCHOOLS—MR. WYKES.

Odd Numbers	Even Numbers
h655 Callander *ma.*	656 Carey, K.S.
h657 Cunning *ma.*	
ah659 Hervey-Bathurst	658 H. A. Evans, O.S.
h661 Butter	660 Horlick
ah663 Pelham	662 Bowman
h665 Strickland	664 Elger-Grogan
s667 Edmondson	666 J. Hildyard
s669 Hodsoll	668 Cohen
as671 Rydon *ma.*	670 Cutting
as673 Pelham-Clinton	672 Gell
s675 J. Dugdale	674 Gill
s677 Watney *ma.*	676 Pixley
as679 J. Peacock	678 Mander
s681 Beech	680 T. Gurney
s683 J. Findlay	682 Somers Cocks
	684 Jenner Fust

ROOM No. 4, WARRE SCHOOLS—MR. MONEY.

s685 Fiennes *ma.*	686 J. Brocklebank
s687 Ingleby	688 Erskine *mi.*
s689 M. Foster	690 Colman
s691 Huntington Whiteley	692 M. Henderson
s693 Macdonald	694 Lascelles
s695 Moon	696 Courage *mi.*
s697 J. Charrington	698 D. Whaley
as699 Prescot	700 Meade Waldo
s701 Wemyss	702 W. Dugdale
s703 Mr. Strutt	704 Thorpe
s705 Lumley-Smith	706 Price
	708 J. Shephard
	710 Birkbeck *mi.*
	712 D. Maitland
	714 Carritt, K.S.
	κ716 Hardinge

E
ROOM No. 5, WARRE SCHOOLS—MR. ALLSOPP.

Odd Numbers	Even Numbers
b727 Hall	κ718 Mackenzie *mi.*
b729 C. Wiggin	κ720 M. Marriott
b731 Coats *mi.*	κ722 Hargreaves
b733 R. Lubbock	κ724 Bradshaw
b735 C. Lindsay	κ726 R. James
b737 Doyle	κ728 Blackett Ord *mi.*
b739 Baer	κ730 Lyon
b741 Burnett-Stuart	κ732 Kidston
b743 Spears	κ734 N. Cayzer
b745 Homfray	κ736 Sir R. Anstruther
b747 Viscount Stuart	κ738 Mr. Cornwallis
b749 Steel	κ740 Drake
b751 Birchenough *ma.*	κ742 Lord Ossulston
	κ744 P. Egerton
	κ746 Cannan
	κ748 R. Furse
	κ750 R. Charrington

h History for Greek.   s Science for Greek.   κ Do Latin only.   a Greek for Latin.   b=E 1.

INSTRUCTIONS TO MASTERS IN TRIALS

A. THE TRIALS OFFICE will be No. 3 New Schools.

(1) Invigilating Masters will call at the Office on their way to their rooms, to fetch the papers which are to be done.

(2) At the end of school, they will at once bring the boys' answers to the Office, after arranging them correctly.

(3) Any difficulty should be referred to the Trials Office.

B. INVIGILATION IN SCHOOLROOMS.

(1) Masters will see that the instructions printed on the boys' blotting-paper are rigidly observed ; these state which books are allowed to be used in doing a paper ; all other literature must be removed.

(2) At the end of the time allotted, the answers must be collected and arranged in their proper piles, and brought to the Trials Office at once. The Blocks must be kept in separate piles ; and if a paper is divided into two or more 'Parts', each 'Part' should also be in a separate pile, unless other instructions are given ; if a paper is divided into 'sections' or portions labelled A B, α β, these should *not* be separated. In each pile, the papers must be arranged in order of the boys' numbers, the lowest number on top. On the top of each pile should be a spare sheet showing (a) Number of room, (b) Number and Part of the Paper, (c) Names of boys absent, with their Numbers.

(3) If a boy completely omits any Paper or Part, he must show up a sheet on which is written his name, number and the word 'Nil'.

(4) Boys are not allowed to leave their room until five minutes before the end of the time allotted ; if they have finished the Paper before this, they may be allowed to show up and then read a suitable book, approved by the Invigilator.

(5) No marks can be given for any answers shown up by a boy after the Papers have been collected.

C. LOOKING OVER PAPERS.

(1) Marks should be entered on the Mark-slip provided, and sent as soon as possible in the special envelope to 'The Accountant'. Speed is especially necessary in the case of the latest papers ; the head of the Block may ask for these marks to be sent direct to his own house.

(2) If a boy's Paper is missing, the Examiner should at once make enquiries, consulting the Invigilator, boy's Tutor, Correctors of other Parts of the Paper, Trials Office, etc.

(3) Entries should be made on the Mark-slip of *Nil*, or o, or *abs.* if a boy shows up *Nil*, or scores no marks, or is shown as *absent* on the covering sheet.

(4) When Trials are over, the bundles of answers may be retained as scribbling paper, or sent to the School Office.

RULES TO BE OBSERVED IN TRIALS

1. Write on one side of the Paper only, and take care not to write beyond the red Line on the right side of the Paper.

2. Begin each question on a new line.

3. If Papers are divided into parts, begin each part on a new Sheet, and show up each part separately, except in Mathematics ; in Mathematics fasten both parts together.

4. Write on the top sheet of your Paper your *Name* and *Number*. Write the Number of the Examination Paper under the Letter which is printed in the right-hand corner.

5. If you do not do any Paper or part of a Paper show up a blank sheet for each part with name and number duly entered and the word 'Nil' written across it.

6. Pay particular attention to any Directions which may be given on the Examination Paper.

7. See that you have the paper or papers intended for you. No allowance can be made for parts of papers omitted, or for work done in papers or in parts of papers not intended for you.

8. No marks can be given for any work shown up after the papers have been collected.

IMPORTANT.

A. All books, pamphlets, notes, etc., brought into school must be put by boys in the place assigned by the Master invigilating.

B. Boys must not have on or about them any matter bearing on the paper being done.

C. Each sheet when completed must be turned face downwards.

D. Any dishonesty in Trials renders a boy liable to lose his remove. This applies to a boy giving as well as to a boy receiving information.

TRIALS MARKS—*Summer* 1936

Masters are requested to enter clearly (1) *above, the number of the Paper under the letter in the right-hand corner, and* (2) *below, the description of the Paper* (e.g. *Algebra, Seen, or Unseen Translation*), *and the Part or Parts for which Marks are appended.*
N.B.—*Enter Marks for each boy exactly opposite his name.*

Full Marks............

Paper.................   Part............

303 E. Lindsay, O.S.		ah507 J. Henderson *mi.*	
305 McWatters, K.S.		h509 Curtis *ma.*	
307 Ashcroft, K.S.		h511 Marsham	
309 Elliott, K.S.		h513 M. Harvey	
311 Onslow, K.S.		h515 P. Roberts	
313 Bourne *mi.* K.S.		h517 Morant	
315 Thomson, K.S.		ah519 Mr. Mackay	
317 D. Mitchell		h521 Peyton Jones	
319 Bland, K.S.		h523 Heywood-Lonsdale	
321 O. K. Heywood		525 Sir A. Meyer, O.S.	
323 Brace		527 Jeudwine	
325 Mr. Neville *mi.*		529 H. Stanley	
327 C. Garton		531 Wrightson	
329 Cory Wright		533 C. W. O. Parker	

h History for Greek.   *a* Greek for Latin.

Signed.......................

N.B.—**Send in Marks, as soon as possible, in the printed envelope provided, addressed to the 'Accountant, School Office'.**
Send in Papers looked over to School Office.
If it is found necessary to alter figures, please REPEAT THE NUMBER IN THE MARGIN so as to avoid errors.

The two columns continue to Nos. 505 and 705 respectively. The block contains odd numbers only—see p. 264.

No.	Papers.	Max.	1	2	3	Total
	Latin Prose .... (or Greek Prose)	100	30	50	20	
11	Verses	100				
	h, s Grammar	50				
3	Latin Translation ...... (or Greek Translation)	100				
8	Unseens .... (h, s ½ French Sent.)	100				
2	History and Geography	100				
12	Divinity	100				
	Total I.	600			Obtained...	
	h, s ...	550				
7	Greek Composition ... h (1) Essay, (2) Map... s Chemistry	100				
10	Greek Translation ...... h Imp. Hist. .... s Pract. Sci. II	100	s Chem.	s Physics		
*& 4	Science..................... Greek h Latin Trans. ... s Physics	100				
	Total II.	300			Obtained ...	

			Repr. 25	Uns. 25	Bk. 50	Comp. 50
5	French	150				
1) 9} 6)	Mathematics	200	Elem. I.	Elem. II.	Addnl.	
	Extra Books (not more than 2 books may be taken). 1 {Homer ....100 French ....100 Math. I ....100 2 {Virgil ....100 German ....100 Math. II ....100 3 {Science ....100 English 80	200				
	General Total	1450				
	h, s ...	1400			Obtained...	

GLOSSARY

OF TERMS PECULIAR TO ETON USED IN THE BOOK

Absence. Calling over or roll call. Called by masters in desk. Each boy as his name is called raises his hat and answers, 'Here, sir !'

Almanack. Gives the calendar for the Half with dates of the principal events.

Bill. 1. List of boys wanted by the Headmaster for any breach of rules.

2. List of teams, crews, etc., excused an Absence.

Block. 1. Swishing block.

2. One of the six main sections, A to F, into which the school is divided.

Business. The school work done on any day. Mostly used of the exchange of Thursday's and Friday's work before the Eton and Harrow Match, expressed by saying that 'Thursday will be Friday's business'. See also *Private* and *Public Business.*

Calendar. Book, published each Half, containing (*a*) complete school list showing each boy's house and tutor, (*b*) arrangement of classes for all subjects, (*c*) school rules and regulations, (*d*) general information, with map.

Cannon Yard. The forecourt of the New Schools.

Captain of the Oppidans. The top Oppidan. His name stands eleventh in school order, the first ten being College Sixth Form.

Captain of the School. The top Colleger.

Chambers. 1. A room at the end of the colonnade in the School Yard where the Headmaster interviews boys officially.

2. A daily meeting of all masters, which used to take place in this room, but now in Upper School.

Choices. 1. Lists of the boys who represent the school at rowing or any game, or their house at football, and of the next dozen or so in order of merit.

2. Lower Boat and Novice Choices are similar lists of the most promising oars in and outside the list of Boats, but none of these represent the school in any competition.

Classical Tutor. A classical master responsible for the work of his pupils and, to some extent, for their general conduct, though in this respect subordinate to the housemaster. A classical housemaster is usually the classical tutor of the boys in his house. As a rule, until he specialises in some non-classical subject, a boy is looked after by the same classical tutor throughout his school career.

Colleger. One of the seventy boys on the Foundation. These have won Entrance Scholarships which entitle them to such reduction of fees as their circumstances require. They board together in the College buildings.

Conduct. A clergyman whose duty it is to take the services in the College Chapel.

Dame. 1. One of the ladies at whose houses boys used to board. Such houses no longer exist.

2. The matron of a master's house.

3. A non-classical housemaster. In this sense the word has long been obsolete.

Desk. Each week about a dozen masters, chosen in rotation, are responsible for attendance in Chapel, for calling Absence and for any special duties required for purposes of discipline. During their week of office they are said to be 'in desk'. Their names are printed in the Almanack.

Division. 1. A class or form of boys taught together in any subject.

2. One of the thirty or more sections into which the school list is divided. A boy's place in the school is known by the number of his division.

Domine. A man who had a boarding house without being a master. Such houses no longer exist.

GLOSSARY

Extra Books. Books on various subjects for boys to prepare voluntarily in their spare time. Papers are set on them in the middle of each Half, and the marks of those who get 40 per cent. or over are counted in the total marks for Trials.

Extra Studies. Four school periods in the week in which boys who have got school certificates are given a considerable choice of subjects outside the range of their ordinary curriculum.

Extra Work. A mathematical exercise set by the mathematical division master, and done out of school.

Extras. Work done with a master out of school hours in any subject that a boy wishes to strengthen. Three hours a week is the normal amount. The small additional sum paid for each boy's Extras is covered by the inclusive fee.

Field. 1. The ground between the Fives Courts and the Slough Road on which school football matches and matches for the House Football Cup are played.

2. Those eventually chosen to make up the School Football Eleven are said to have 'got their Field'.

First Hundred. The top block of Fifth Form, containing nowadays some 150 or 160 boys. Except for the twenty boys in Sixth Form it is the top block of the school.

Form. Synonymous with a block, but only used with the ordinal numbers from Third to Sixth.

Georgic. One of Virgil's *Georgics* written out as a punishment.

Half. A term or schooltime.

History Questions. Answers written out of school to questions on history set by the division master.

House Tutor. The master in charge of a boys' house. The title was originally confined to classical housemasters, the non-classical ones being the dames of boys in their houses ; but this distinction disappeared at the end of the nineteenth century.

Jordan. The lower part of Colenorton Brook, running between the Drawing Schools, Racket Courts and Field

271

on the one side, and Mesopotamia and the piece of ground also called Jordan on the other, and then under Fifteen Arch Bridge into the river at Sixth Form Bench.

Judy's Passage. The passage from the Dorney Road to the space in front of New Schools between Cotton Hall House and Waynflete at one end, and Common Lane House and Holland House at the other. Two branches now run to the Slads and the Drill Hall Schools respectively.

Keeper. Used instead of captain in certain games—Keeper of the Field, of the Fives, etc. There are usually a keeper and a second keeper.

Long Lie. No early school.

Long Walk. 1. The space between Upper School and the roadway.

2. The road from the Castle to the equestrian statue of George III.

Lord's. The annual cricket match against Harrow.

Lower Boy. A boy in Remove or Fourth Form, who has to fag. In College a boy in his first year, whatever part of the school he is in.

Lower Master. The master in charge of Remove, Fourth Form and Third Form, and of Lower Chapel, who, in case of the Headmaster's absence, acts as his deputy.

Mark in (out). To make a list of absentees from school, Chapel, etc. In school this is done by the master or some boy appointed by him ; in Chapel by the boy at the end of each pew, the lists being collected before service begins and given to masters in desk. All lists are subsequently checked at the School Office. The old term was *Mark in*, but *Mark out* is now more usual.

Modern Tutor. A non-classical master who is responsible for boys specialising in modern subjects just as a classical tutor is for those doing classics.

Non-dies. A day on which there is no regular work.

Oppidan. Any boy who is not a Colleger.

Order. 1. An order to a shop to supply a boy with specified goods. This may be given by a housemaster (or his dame) or by parents.

2. The order of merit in a boy's various divisions.

3. A ration of bread, butter, tea, milk and sugar supplied in houses for boys' teas—formerly for breakfast also.

Passing. The test in swimming which boys are required to pass before they are allowed on the river. For details see *Eton Book of the River*, pp. 38–40.

Porny School. The Eton elementary school. See p. 38.

Private Business. Work done with a boy's classical or modern tutor at the discretion of the tutor and outside the boy's school work.

Provost. Head of the College, elected by the Fellows on a *congé d'élire* from the Crown, holds office till resignation or death, expected to be in residence during termtime. He has control, constitutionally absolute and virtually considerable, over Chapel and the domestic arrangements of the College.

Public Business. Any work connected with regular school—now obsolete.

Pupil Room. (*a*) The room, usually not a schoolroom, in which a tutor teaches his pupils. (*b*) The work done or the time spent in pupil room.

Reading Over. At the end of each schooltime the results of Trials, and, in the summer, of the examination for First Hundred, are read over in Upper School by the Headmaster for upper boys, by the Lower Master for lower boys.

Remove. Block E, or the fifth block in the school. It usually contains 200 or more boys, and no boy may remain in it after the age of 16. Spelt with *R* in text.

Remove. (*a*) A group of boys who, if they pass in Trials, are promoted together each schooltime. There are normally three removes in each block. (*b*) The distance traversed in promotion : 'he loses his remove', 'he gains a double remove'. Spelt with *r* in text.

St. Mark's School. A school in Windsor, now known as the Imperial Service College.

GLOSSARY

Second Sine. Second house football eleven.

Sixpenny. Summer title of a cricket field between the Slough Road and the Fives Courts. Called at other seasons the Field.

Sock. (*a*) Almost anything to eat, but especially sweet-stuff. (*b*) To sock, to consume sock. (*c*) To make a present ; *e.g.* I'll sock you sixpence.

Staying out. Excused school owing to illness.

Sunday Private. A short lesson or talk, given by tutors to pupils on Sunday.

Sunday Questions. Questions set by division masters and the written answers to them done by boys on Sunday.

Tardy Book. Book kept at the School Office in which unpunctual boys have to enter their names before early school.

Theme. Latin free composition on a subject set by the tutor and done in pupil room. Abolished by Dr. Hornby in favour of Latin prose done in school.

Timbralls. (*a*) Name of the house immediately south of the Field or Sixpenny. (*b*) Official name of the Field or Sixpenny.

Trials. Examination of all boys held at the end of each Half.

Tug. A Colleger.

Tutor. (*a*) At the beginning of the period a title reserved for classical masters who took pupils and for those masters as housemasters. (*b*) Later extended to all masters taking pupils. (*c*) And also to all masters holding houses.

Vice-Provost. Acts as Provost in the latter's absence. Elected by the Provost and Fellows from among present Fellows or former assistant masters. Since the Public Schools Commission no other ex-assistant master has become a Fellow.

Wall. (*a*) The wall extending from Weston's to Fifteen Arch Bridge serving as boundary between the Slough Road and College Field. Against it the Wall football game is played. (*b*) The low wall in front of Upper School between the Long Walk and the street.

INDEX

ABSENCE, calling, 43, 46, 47, 59
Academicals, 36
Accommodation. *See* Boarding Houses
Acting, 103, 104
Admission, ages of, 157
Agar's Plough, 233
Agriculture, 88
Ainger, A. C., 199
Albert, Prince Consort, 173, 174
Alington, Dr., 38, 52, 80–86, 90, 108, 181
Ampthill, Lord, 238
Angelo's, 191
Annals of an Eton House, by Major Gambier-Parry, 140
Archaeological Society, the, 250
Archery, 232
Architecture, 189
Arms, School of, 191
Army Class, 75, 88
Askew-Robertson, W. H., 193, 194
Athletic Sports, 238
Austen-Leigh, R. A., 127, 172, 177

BADEN-POWELL, General (Lord), 224
Baker, Captain A. C., 64, 66, 245
Baldwin's Shore, 198
Balston, Dr., 148, 182, 183
Barnby, Sir Joseph, 86, 107, 180
Baths, 214
Beagles, 217, 218, 236
Benson, Dr. A. C., 173
Biology, 88
Birdcage, 196
Bird Sanctuary, 251
Bland, H. M., 251
Block System, 157 ff.
Boarding Houses, 32, 42, 84, 126 ff., 153, 200, 201

Book Pound, 243, 246
Bookshop, 189
Boredom, boys', 112, 113
Boringdon, Viscount, 181
Boxing, 109, 191, 239
Browning, Oscar, 34
Buckley, Major R. M., 246
Buildings, Lists of, 201, 204–209
Bullying, 142
Bunker's, 244
Burne-Jones, Sir E., 176

CALDWELL, J. H., 195
Calendar, the, 66–69
'Call', 47
Cambridge, 75, 79, 115
Camps, 222
Carpentry, 100, 101, 109
Carter, Rev. T. B., 175, 191
Carter, Rev. W. A., 51, 203
Carter, Rev. W. M., 252
Carter House, 189
Carter's Passage, 199
Caxton Schools, 192
Cecil, Lord Hugh, 86
Cercle français, Le, 250
Chamber, John, 68
Chapel as Parish Church, 197
Chapel, services and attendance, 42, 45, 69, 85, 86, 107, 149, 171 ff., 177, 183, 186, 196, 210, 220
Chapman, E. W., 220
Chemical Laboratory, 199
Chemistry, 88, 89
Christopher, the, 189
Clark-Kennedy, A. W. M., 251
Classics, 31, 39, 53, 70, 71, 75, 80, 81, 87, 91, 92, 117–119, 122, 123, 154, 169, 170, 257 ff.
Cloisters, 197
Clubs, Sports, 235

Coleridge, Rev. Edward, 172, 179
Collections, 70, 167
Collegers, 31, 40, 41, 42, 55, 56, 57, 161, 210
Common Lane House, 190
Concentration, mental, 26
Corps, 59, 72, 220 ff.

'DAME' defined, 127
Dames' Houses, 32, 33, 42, 43, 126 ff., 146
Darwin, Robert, 106
Day-boys, 128
Debating Societies, 251
Derivations, 150
Devon, Lord, 212
Discipline, 43, 44, 115, 143
Divinity, 75, 78, 169
Domines, 126 ff.
Dormitories, 134, 144
Drawing, 100, 103
Drawing Schools, 192, 193
Dress, school, 211 ff.
Drill Hall, 192
Drury's, 190
Duclos, M., 38
Dupuis, G. H., 66, 67
Dupuis, Henry, 178
Durnford, F. E., 181
Durnford House, 190
Dutchman's Farm, 233

EDUCATION, 79, 111 ff., 116, 117, 254 ff.
Elliott, C. A., 86
Elvey, Dr., 179
English, school subject, 28, 93, 124, 125
Equipment, present day, 207–210
Essay Society, the, 250
Essay writing, 93, 94
Essays, Latin, 149
Essex, R. H., 173
Etiquette, 214
Eton College Chronicle, the, 59, 225, 231, 233

INDEX

Eton College Guide, by R. A. Austen-Leigh, 172, 177, 184
Eton College Rifle Volunteers, 59, 72, 220 ff.
Eton Mission, the, 252
Eton Society, the, 249
Etoniana, by R. A. Austen-Leigh, 127
Evans, Jane, 106, 129
Evans, Samuel (I), 105
Evans, Samuel (II), 106, 222
Evans, Sidney, 106
Evans, William, 105, 140
Evans', 105
Examinations, 70, 71. *See* Trials
Examiners, how appointed, 170
'Extra Masters', 42
'Extra Studies', 74, 108

FAGGING, 30, 142, 143
Fees, concerning, 74, 75, 83, 137, 138, 146, 147, 148
Fencing, 191, 239
Film Society, the, 250
Finances, concerning, 82 ff., 89, 137, 203, 204, 237
First Hundred Examination, 170
Fives Courts, 193, 194, 199, 236
Football, 141, 225–227, 240
Ford, Rev. Lionel 243
Forms, names of, 29
French, 37, 38, 45, 75, 76, 87, 121, 123
'Fusee, the', 63

GAFFNEY, Sergeant-Major, 66
Gambier-Parry, Major, 140
Games and Sports, 225 ff.
Geography, 97, 125
German, 70, 71, 75, 124. *See also* Modern Languages
Gladstone, W. E., 57
Godsal, Major P. T., 223
Golf, 239, 240
Goodford, Dr., 37, 51, 127, 148, 182

Gosling, E. L., 193
Governing Body, the, 48, 50, 57
Gramophone Society, the, 107, 250
Great War Memorial, 184
Greek, 76, 122. *See also* Classics
Grenfell, Francis, 237
Grenfell, Riversdale, 237
Gulliver's, 189, 202
Gymnasium, 109, 191, 192, 239
Gymnastics, 239

HACKNEY WICK, 252
Hale, Edward, 37
Hall, A. H., 178
Hall, William, 63
Hanbury, Major Evan, 193
Handicrafts, 102
Hats, 212, 219
Hatton's, 239
Hawtrey, J. W., 29
Hawtrey, Dr. Stephen, 36, 41, 187
Hawtrey House, 190
Hawtrey Library, 196
Hayne, Dr., 179, 180
Headmasters, duties of, 42, 43, 46, 59, 73, 80, 86, 132, 135
Heath, George, 126
Hibbert, John, 52
Higher (School) Certificate, 168, 169, 170
Hill, M. D., 251
Historical Geography, 97, 125
History, 71, 75, 76, 78, 96, 121, 123, 125, 169, 170
History of Eton College, by Sir H. Maxwell-Lyte, 126, 127
Hockey, 239
Hodgson, Dr., 36, 173
Hodgson House, 189, 190, 198
Holidays, 69
Holland House, 200
Hollway-Calthrop, Mr., 192, 203
Hopgarden, 191
Hornby, Dr., 31 ff., 54, 128, 142, 149, 169, 252
Housemasters, 44, 45, 131 ff., 153, 154

Houses. *See* Boarding Houses, and under separate names

JAMES, Dr. M. R., 171, 173, 186
Jiu-jitsu, 239
Johnson, William, 146, 181
Johnson, Dr., 180
Jourdelay's, 189, 198
Judy's Passage, 199, 200
Junior School, abolished, 45

KEATE HOUSE, 198
Kingsmen, 31, 41
Kynaston, Canon Herbert, 178

LABORATORIES, 89
Laleham Preparatory School, 12 ff.
Land Prizes, 88
Latin, 76, 149–150. *See also* Classics
Laundry, 195, 243
Lawn Tennis, 239, 240
Leave System, 66, 69, 70, 74
Leave Ticket, 62
Lemoine, M., 38
L'Estrange, Rev. A. G., 239
Ley, Dr. H., 86, 108, 180
Library, 190, 247
Library, Hawtrey, 196
Library, house, 140
Lists, 67
Literati, the, 249
Literature, 95–96, 104
Little Brown's, 244
Lloyd, Dr. C. H., 107, 180
Long Wall, 196
Lower Chapel, 183–186, 199
Lower School, 29, 30
Luddington, James, 88
Luxmoore, H. E., 176, 177, 198
Lyte, Sir H. Maxwell-, 126, 127, 142
Lyttelton, Dr., 41, 52, 73 ff., 88, 192
Lyttelton, Lord, 51, 212

MACLEAN, Dr., 180
Manor House, 190

Masters, assistant, 40, 41, 44, 45, 73, 80, 81, 128 ff.
Mathematical Schools, 198
Mathematics, 34, 35, 36, 38, 39, 40, 44, 45, 71, 74, 75, 76, 79, 87, 120, 123, 165, 169, 170, 259
Matron and Nurses, 145
Maude, John, 32, 214, 249
Mayall, A., 251
Mechanics, School of, 192
Memoirs, by John Maude, 32, 249
Menzies-Jones, Frederick, 106
Merrick's, 244
Mesopotamia, 233
Metal Work, 100, 101, 109
'Methods' of Teaching, 255, 256
Modern Languages, 37, 70, 71, 74, 165, 169, 170
Montague James Schools, 199
Morley, Earl of, 52
Mullens, Sir John, 193
Museum, 190, 199
Music, 100, 102, 103, 105–109, 187
Music, in Chapel, 177–180
Music Schools, 199
Musical Society, the, 108
Mustians, 199, 202, 203
Myers, Major W. J., 223

NAME-CARVING, 63, 64
Natural History Society, the, 250, 251
Natural Science, 87
New Boys, 158–161
New Schools, 32

OFFICERS' TRAIN-ING CORPS, 101, 102, 109, 223–224
Okes, Rev. R., 51
Old Choristers' Associa-tion, 108
Oppidans, 43, 55, 128
Osborne, Sergeant-Major, 59, 66
O.T.C., 223
Oxford, 75, 79, 115

PAINTING, 100
Passings, 72
Paul, Kegan, 181
Penn House, 190, 200
Pensions, 83
Photographic Society, the, 250
Physical Training, 100, 101, 102, 109
Physics, 88, 89
Picture Gallery, 192, 252
Play acting, 104, 248
Political Society, the, 250
'Pop', 213, 215, 219, 247, 249
Porny, Anthony, 38
Postmasterships, 68
Powell, E. W., 106, 224, 251
Powell, Joby, 243
Praepostors, 47, 60, 61, 62
Praepostors, Head-master's, 62
Prajadhipok, King, 196
Preachers, 180
Précis-writing, 94, 95
Preparatory Schools :
  Arithmetic, 27
  Baths, 7, 13
  Chilblains, 10
  Common Entrance Ex-amination, 158
  Food, 4, 5, 7, 12
  French, 15
  Games, 5, 6, 13
  General Knowledge, 25–26
  Gymnasium, 6
  Laleham, school at, 12 ff.
  Music, 10
  'Pig-table', 5
  Prize Task, 16
  Punishments, 5, 6, 8, 9, 11, 15, 16
  Rewards, 7, 8, 9
  Richmond, school at, 3 ff.
  Sanitation, 14
  Subjects taught, 7, 8
  Sundays, 7
Prideaux, Captain Geof-frey, 193
Prizes, 34, 35, 88, 170
Profession, choice of, 104, 105
Promotion, in school, 70, 159–161, 167

Property, of the College, 82 ff., 130
Provost, duty of, 52
Provost, appointed by the Crown, 187
Provost's Lodge, 196
Punch, 58
Punishments, 60 ff.
Pyron du Martre, M. Antoine. *See* Porny, Anthony

QUEEN'S SCHOOLS, 183, 199

RACKET COURTS, 194, 239, 240
Ramsay, A. B., 186, 224
Recreation, 242
Religious Instruction, 147
Renier, M., 80
Report Forms, 62
Richmond Preparatory School, 3 ff.
Rickards, Sir G. K., 52
Rifle-shooting, 109, 220, 221, 224
Roberts, W. H., 127
Rotunda, 198
Rowing, 141, 236
Rowland's, 244
Royal Commission Re-port on Public Schools, 35, 36, 47 ff., 53, 57, 146–148, 180, 202
Rushworth, Sergeant-Major, 245
Russian, 124

SALARIES, Masters', 35, 36, 135
Sanatorium, 144, 145, 191
Scholarships, 170
School Certificate, 71, 75, 89, 94, 115, 167, 168
School Clerk, 64
School Hall, 190, 247, 248
School Hours, 44, 47, 58
School Lists, 33, 45
School of Arms, 191
School of Mechanics, 192
School Office, 59, 63, 64, 66, 70
School Stores, 243, 245
Schooltimes, 68, 157, 158

INDEX

Science, 38, 39, 44, 45, 71, 74, 75, 79, 87, 88, 90, 98, 114, 121, 169, 170, 259
Scientific Society, the, 250
Scott, Rev. Robert, 51
Scouts, Boy, 220, 224
Sermons, 181-182
Shakespeare Society, the, 250
Singh, Prince Duleep, 193
Sir Galahad, by G. F. Watts, 176-177
Sixpenny, 194, 230, 231, 233
Sock shops, 243, 244
Solly, Edward, 38
Soltau-Symons, Major, 223
South African War Memorial, 177, 190
Specialising, 75, 81, 89, 115, 116
Squash Courts, 194
Stephen, J. K., 189
Sterry, Sir Wasey, 177, 178

Stokes, Sir G. G., 51
Subjects taught, concerning, 74, 148, 155, 156, 257
Sullivan, Sir Arthur, 10
Superannuation, 159

TAPESTRIES, 176, 185
Tardy Book, the, 65, 66
Terms. *See* Schooltimes
Text-books, 114
'Theme', 149
Things Ancient and Modern, by Dr. Alington, 73, 90
Thompson, Rev. W. H., 51
Timbralls. *See* Sixpenny
Times, The, quoted, 54-57
Tomline, George, 35
Trials, 65, 70, 162 ff.
Tristram, Professor E.W., 173
'Tug of Warre, The', 58
Tutorial System, 146 ff.

UPPER SCHOOL, 196

WALL PAINTINGS, in Chapel, 171, 173-174
Wallis, T. H., 246
Walpole House, 199, 203
War Memorials, 177, 184, 190, 197
Warre, Dr., 41, 52, 53 ff., 87, 158, 182, 197, 215, 220, 246, 247, 252
Warre, Edmond, 195
Warre House, 190, 200
Warre Schools, 191
Watts, G. F., 176-177
Waynflete House, 200, 202
Webber's, 244
Welldon, Mr., 54
Westbury House, 200, 202
Weston's Yard, 196
Wilder, Rev. J., 172, 173
Windsor and Eton Choral Society, 248
Windsor Fair incident, 37
Wise, Charlie, 189
Wolley-Dod, 190
Wright, Mat, 244

278